Positive Alternatives to Restraint and Seclusion for Aggressive Kids

Kathleen McConnell

Katherine O. Synatschk

pro·ed
An International Publisher

© 2012 by PRO-ED, Inc.
8700 Shoal Creek Boulevard
Austin, Texas 78757-6897
800/897-3202   Fax 800/397-7633
www.proedinc.com

All rights reserved. **Except as indicated below**, no part of the material protected by this copyright notice may be reproduced or used in any form or by any means, electronic or mechanical, including photocopying, recording, or by any information storage and retrieval system, without prior written permission of the copyright owner.

This product includes a CD with reproducible pages.

Limited Photocopy License
PRO-ED, Inc. grants to individual purchasers of this material nonassignable permission to reproduce the handouts in the text and the electronic version of the Student Intervention Plan and all forms and activities on the CD. This license is limited to you, the individual purchaser, for use with your students or clients on one campus only.

This license does not grant the right to reproduce these materials for resale, redistribution, or any other purposes (including but not limited to books, pamphlets, articles, video- or audiotapes, and handouts or slides for lectures or workshops). Permission to reproduce these materials for these and other purposes must be obtained in writing from the Permissions Department of PRO-ED, Inc.

ISBN-13: 978-1-4164-0446-0

Printed in the United States of America

1   2   3   4   5   6   7   8   9   10   16   15   14   13   12   11

Contents

Acknowledgments		iv
1	**An Overview of Restraint and Seclusion in the Schools**	1
	Basic Interventions	1
	Background	2
	Risks Associated With Using Restraint and Seclusion	3
	Definition of Terms	4
2	**Serious Behavioral Difficulties as Problems of Self-Regulation**	5
	Emotional and Behavioral Dysregulation	5
	Techniques for Calm	7
	The Importance of Relationship in Improving Self-Regulation	9
	Self-Regulation Skills	11
3	**A Model for Positive Alternatives to Restraint and Seclusion**	13
	Referral	13
	Meetings and Conferences	13
	Establishing Goals	14
	Description of the Materials, and Directions for Use	14
	Appendix 3.A: Referral Discussion Guide	21
	Appendix 3.B: Close Monitoring of Behavior	29
4	**Skill Units**	71
	Skill Unit 1: Describes physical sensations separately from emotions	73
	Skill Unit 2: Expresses emotions verbally	89
	Skill Unit 3: Accepts criticism and praise	95
	Skill Unit 4: Takes responsibility for actions	101
	Skill Unit 5: Initiates a calming strategy after being upset	111
	Skill Unit 6: Follows directions from adults	127
	Skill Unit 7: Responds to nonverbal cues	137
	Skill Unit 8: Demonstrates empathy for others	143
	Skill Unit 9: Works productively in a group	149
	Skill Unit 10: Identifies consequences before acting	155
	Skill Unit 11: Manages transitions	165
	Skill Unit 12: Uses resources for obtaining help when getting upset	175
	Skill Unit 13: Attends to task, ignores distractions	183
	Skill Unit 14: Respects personal boundaries, rights, and property of others	187
	Skill Unit 15: Negotiates with others when there is disagreement	193
References		199
About the Authors		203

Acknowledgments

Kathleen McConnell

I would like to express my thanks to all of the many administrators, teachers, counselors, and support personnel whose dedication and hard work with the most challenging students is greatly appreciated. I admire them and what they do.

Katherine O. Synatschk

I want to thank all of the students in my life, from graduate students in counseling to students served in special education, for teaching me over and over again that collaboration and a focus on what works is the way to go.

Chapter 1
An Overview of Restraint and Seclusion in the Schools

Educators, parents, and advocates have voiced concerns about the use of restraint and seclusion, even with students who demonstrate dangerous, aggressive, and threatening behaviors. Specific concerns about using restraint and seclusion techniques with students who have disabilities have resulted in the adoption of local and state laws, policies, and regulations that limit their use.

Positive Alternatives to Restraint and Seclusion for Aggressive Kids provides resources for educators who work with schools' most challenging students. Defiant, aggressive, out of control, and violent students put everyone at risk. These students may harm themselves, other students, or adults in educational settings. Everyone in a school should feel safe, and when students compromise their own safety or that of others, educators must take action.

Basic Interventions

In response to violence and aggression, educators must include well-planned and practiced responses to crises. All educators should be taught crisis intervention procedures, and every campus should have a crisis intervention team ready and willing to intervene when a student loses control and is a danger to him- or herself or others. Several well-known and reputable crisis prevention and intervention programs are available, and schools should implement at least one of these programs and provide staff members with initial and updated training.

Have a school code of conduct that clearly articulates the positive and negative consequences of students' actions in the educational setting. The consequences can address issues such as attendance; tardiness; misbehavior in class and in common areas of the school; bus behavior; serious incidents of fighting, bullying, drug or alcohol possession and use; weapons possession; and other behavioral issues common to schools. Prescribe school policies that define the positive consequences in place when students behave well along with consequences that are intended to reduce misbehavior, especially when students' misbehavior is serious and disruptive to the learning environment. It is helpful to have a clear continuum of consequences that ranges from mild to severe, depending on the nature and impact of the misbehavior, and mild to highly rewarding for the positive, desirable behaviors.

Positive Alternatives to Restraint and Seclusion for Aggressive Kids is not intended to replace a school's crisis prevention or intervention plan, nor is it intended to bypass the established code of conduct and continuum of consequences. Rather, it provides education professionals with tools for students who continue to exhibit serious, disruptive, and sometimes dangerous behaviors that result in serious responses, such as the use of restraint and seclusion. These students, who are usually few in number but who often demand a disproportionate amount of educators' time, require unique and targeted interventions. Typical behavior interventions do not work with them; their behaviors are extreme and outside the boundaries of low-level, group interventions.

Effective interventions for the most challenging students must be targeted to their specific needs, which are often different from the needs of other students. The most challenging students need to learn skills that are often basic and difficult to teach; key self-regulation skills involve self-awareness, self-control, and self-management. Competencies such as recognizing when one is upset, knowing how to calm down when agitated, expressing empathy for others, and following rules are examples of important skills that the most challenging students often lack.

Teaching these skills does not usually fit into large-group academic instruction. Consequently, administrators, teachers, counselors, behavior specialists, and others who target these skills for instruction require a smaller instructional setting, time away from academic instruction, and commitment to a process that takes time. It is possible, however, that such efforts will be successful and that, over the long term, the challenging student will learn important and needed prosocial skills. Thus, the student demands less time from teachers, counselors, administrators, and others because his or her behavior will improve and will no longer require immediate post-incident responses.

The next section provides background information related to the issue of restraint and seclusion in educational settings. Restraint and seclusion, especially when used with students who have disabilities, is an emotionally charged issue for every educational constituency—administrators, teachers, counselors, support personnel, parents, advocates, and the students themselves. Providing effective tools that will improve the behavior of challenging students so that restraint and seclusion are used only when absolutely necessary is important in order to reduce the threat of violence and aggression. Alternatives to the use of restraint and seclusion also reduce the risk of harm to everyone in the educational environment. When restraint and seclusion are limited in frequency and duration, educators and students can focus on the business of school, which is teaching and learning, not physical intervention and management.

Background

Ryan, Peterson, Tetreault, and van der Hagen (2007) have provided an historical perspective on the use of restraint and seclusion. Descriptions of restraint can be found in the literature as early as the 1950s, when physical restraint was suggested as a means to prevent damage or injury when students began to lose control. Later literature mentioned restraint as one of many intervention techniques that are part of classroom management options. While chemical and mechanical restraints have been used in some settings, restraint in educational settings is typically physical rather than chemical or mechanical. The authors point out that seclusion has an even longer history in school settings and has included inclusion and exclusion.

In January 2009, the National Disability Rights Network (NDRN) released an investigative report called *School Is Not Supposed to Hurt: Investigative Report on Abusive Restraint and Seclusion in Schools*. The report documented numerous and sometimes shocking examples of the misuse of restraint and seclusion, including instances of students suffocating to death after being put in prone restraints or being locked in seclusion rooms for hours at a time. The report indicated that seclusions and restraints were sometimes used not as responses to crises or to prevent physical injury or danger but rather as punishment.

The report also described the work of the Protection and Advocacy (P&A) system, which protects the rights of children and adults with disabilities. The P&A network provides legally based advocacy services to people with disabilities in the United States. A second section of the NDRN report was a description of best practices in education, including the use of positive behavioral supports, to reduce the use of restraint and seclusion. While restraint and seclusion have been described in the literature, guidelines for their use have been limited and, in some states, nonexistent. The NDRN findings indicated that 41% of states had no laws, policies, or guidelines concerning restraint and seclusion use in their schools.

The NDRN report, and media reports of harm done to children in schools because of the use of restraint and seclusion, have attracted the attention of officials in the Department of Education as well as of state and local officials. On July 31, 2009, the Secretary of Education sent a letter to the states and territories urging them to develop, review, or revise their state policies and guidelines to ensure that every student under its jurisdiction was protected from unnecessary or inappropriate restraint or seclusion. The secretary further suggested that the states disseminate information to administrators, teachers, and parents to ensure that everyone understood the guidelines as well as the resources available that related to restraint and seclusion. The Office of Elementary and Secondary Education was assigned the task of working with regional staff to help states develop or revise their state laws, regulations, policies, and guidance.

The United States Department of Education's 2009 report titled *Summary of Seclusion and Restraint Statutes, Regulations, Policies and Guidance, by State and Territory: Information as Reported to the Regional Comprehensive Centers and Gathered From Other Sources* detailed (1) the statutes and regulations addressing seclusion and restraint; (2) policies and guidance addressing seclusion and restraint; and (3) currently developing or revising state statutes, regulations, policies, or guidance on a state-by-state basis. This report indicates that there is no consistency among states and territories regarding the use of restraint of seclusion. Some states have laws, rules, and regulations and some do not. At the time the report was written, 19 states had no laws at all. Of the 31 states that did have laws in place, many were not comprehensive enough to protect all students, in every kind of school. A review of the report's contents confirms that most state laws, regulations, and guidelines do not even specify the behaviors that justify or permit the use of restraint and seclusion.

Also in 2009, the House of Representatives passed The Keeping All Students Safe Act (H.R. 4247), which was intended to regulate the use of restraint and seclusion. However, the Senate failed to pass its version of the legislation. Among the components of the bill that were not agreed to related to including restraint and seclusion in Individualized Education Programs (IEPs). Even though Congress failed to pass the restraint and seclusion legislation, some states have begun to develop, review, and revise their own legislation. Some of the changes states have begun to implement include clearly defining terms such as *restraint* and *seclusion*, articulating the conditions under which these techniques can be used, and banning face-down holds and seclusion rooms.

Risks Associated With Using Restraint and Seclusion

The National Disability Rights Network's report summarized some of the results of using restraint and seclusion with students who have disabilities. Because the Department of Education and state education agencies have not required districts to report the use of restraint and seclusion, accurate data related to injuries and deaths of students from the use of restraint and seclusion are not available. However, the Government Accountability Office report (Kutz, 2009) detailed hundreds of alleged cases of the inappropriate use of restraint and seclusion, often by untrained staff. Incidents included the use of ropes, duct tape, and chairs with straps and bungee cords to restrain or isolate students, often young children.

Definition of Terms

In 2000, Congress passed the Children's Health Act, which defined the terms *restraint* and *seclusion*. The Centers of Medicare and Medicaid Services further clarified these definitions when it issued its Conditions for Participation to Hospitals in December 2006 (National Disability Rights Network, 2009).

A restraint was defined as follows:

(A) Any manual method, physical or mechanical device, material, or equipment that immobilizes or reduces the ability of an individual to move his or her arms, legs, body, or head freely; or

(B) A drug or medication when it is used as a restriction to manage the individual's freedom of movement and is not a standard treatment or dosage for the individual's condition.

(C) A restraint does not include devices, such as orthopedically prescribed devices, surgical dressings or bandages, protective helmets, or other method that involve the physical holding of an individual for the purpose of conducting routine physical examinations or tests, or to protect the individual from falling out of bed, or to permit the individual to participate in activities without the risk of physical harm (this does not include a physical escort).

Seclusion was defined as follows: "The involuntary confinement of an individual alone in a room or area from which the individual is physically prevented from leaving." Seclusion may only be used for the management of violent or self-destructive behavior.

Since the publication of the Department of Education report and the passage of the House bill, many states have begun to review their practices related to the use of restraint and seclusion, especially seclusionary time out. States have published technical assistance documents and proposed new policies, laws, regulations, and guidelines. In addition, advocacy groups have written their own reports and collected additional information related to these practices, especially as they related to students with disabilities. At the time of publication of these materials, there has been no further legislative action in the United States Senate or any additional directives from the Department of Education except for reporting requirements.

We believe the use of restraint and seclusion will continue to be discussed and legislated, especially at the state level. Regardless of actions taken legislatively, however, difficult and challenging situations will continue to arise in schools. Educators always need interventions, strategies, tools, and methods for dealing with serious behavior problems. We hope that *Positive Alternatives to Restraint and Seclusion for Aggressive Kids* will be of daily benefit to administrators, teachers, support personnel, and others faced with difficult situations. Students who are dangerous, aggressive, and threatening cannot be ignored, and interventions that work to improve their behavior are essential.

Chapter 2
Serious Behavioral Difficulties as Problems of Self-Regulation

The challenging students whose needs are addressed in this book are referred for aggressive and out-of-control behaviors—problems typically labeled as serious behavioral problems. In the literature, many researchers have begun to define these behaviors as deficits in self-regulation. Students with serious self-regulation difficulties can have an enormous negative impact on the successful functioning of schools and on all the students, teachers, and administrators working there. This book provides strategies to address self-regulation difficulties and develop key social-emotional skills.

Emotional and Behavioral Dysregulation

Self-regulation abilities enable people to know and manage their emotions, recognize emotions in others, and make use of those abilities in relationships. With an adequate capacity for self-regulation, they are able to control an immediate response to stimuli so that they can make choices about how to behave. Self-regulation is key to emotional intelligence and important to school success. Here is a description of a regulated student, contrasted with a student who is dysregulated (Saxe et al., 2007).

The Regulated Student

- Spends most of his or her time in control of emotional responses
- Self-soothes by using internal and external resources
- Reengages in activities and with others with relative ease after he or she has become upset
- Almost never engages in dangerous behavior when stressed

The Dysregulated Student

- Has difficulty controlling his or her emotional states
- Often expresses negative emotions such as anger, fear, shame, guilt, or anxiety
- Has difficulty with self-soothing, returning to calmness, and reengaging with others and with activities after he or she has become upset
- Has intense changes in awareness (consciousness), affect (emotion), action (behavior), and relatedness (sense of connection to others) when faced with a stressor
- Becomes dysregulated at least once a month, causing social, academic, or other problems
- May become behaviorally dysregulated and engage in dangerous behavior if stressed and in the midst of an episode of emotional dysregulation

Students with self-regulation difficulties may either "act out," making it clear there is a problem, or "act in," giving subtle clues that something is wrong (Levine & Kline, 2007). The four symptoms of hyperarousal, dissociation, constriction, and freeze are normal responses to overwhelming experience, but in students with self-regulation difficulties they occur more often than normal and become problematic, enduring symptoms (Perry, 2006). These four symptoms are described here, along with typical behaviors that are associated with them.

Hyperarousal is defined as having greater than normal physiological activation, including breathing and heart rate, and may include the following behaviors:

- Exaggerated emotional response
- Guardedness
- Compulsive talking
- Anxiety and phobia
- Agitation
- Fidgeting
- Darting eyes
- Restless legs
- Distractibility
- Hyperactivity
- Out-of-seat behavior
- Frequent crying and irritability
- Temper tantrums
- Abrupt mood changes
- Looking-for-a-fight and rage reactions
- Increased risk-taking behavior

Dissociation is defined as having a response in which there is disconnect between present awareness and the present physical and emotional experience. The following behaviors are associated with dissociation:

- Daydreaming
- Distractibility and inattentiveness
- Reduced ability to organize and plan
- Feeling easily and frequently stressed out
- Having a blank stare
- Excessive shyness
- Having one's head in the clouds
- Living in an imaginary world
- Inability to connect to others

Constriction is defined as a response in which attention, breathing, muscle tone, and posture constrict. *Freeze* is an automatic response to inescapable extreme stress. Constriction and freeze may include these behaviors:

- Muscle tension
- Fatigue
- Headaches, stomachaches, and other physical complaints
- Feelings of shame and guilt
- Diminished curiosity
- Feelings and behaviors of helplessness

- Eating disorders
- Avoidance behavior

Techniques for Calm

Even students with self-regulation difficulties are in a regulated emotional state most of the time; that is, they are relatively calm, are in control of their emotions, are oriented to the environment, and have continuity in their responses. The "wedge of cognition" technique (Saxe et al., 2007) can help students recognize the physiological and emotional shifts that lead to dysregulation and to use cognition to calm and direct emotional and behavioral responses. Essentially, in a fraction of a second, it helps students reflect on the sensations and emotions they are feeling and to make conscious decisions about what to do next.

Neuroscience research tells us that somatic experience is the way to help kids improve their capacity for self-regulation (van der Kolk, 2006). The goal is to enable children (and caregivers) to recognize, label, and use input from their bodies as a guide to managing their emotions, interrupting dysregulation, and making a wedge of cognition possible. This opens the door to increased executive functioning, which includes adaptive decision making and planning for the future, anticipating the consequences of actions, and inhibiting inappropriate responses. Essential techniques for calming include grounding, mindful awareness, and tracking sensation. The essential resource is the adult's calm, emotionally regulated state.

Grounding

The beginning skill of *grounding* was referred to by Ogden and her colleagues (2006) as a core somatic resource, giving a feeling of both physical and psychological solidity and stability. Grounding affords one a sense of self-support and integrity through the back, legs, and feet and their connection to the ground. Levine and Kline (2007) suggested that grounding gives a kid the feeling of the solid connection to the earth and facilitates being directly connected to his or her body's sensations. There is no right or wrong way to become grounded. For some, simply stopping to take a slow, deep breath and noticing their feet's connection to the floor will work. Grounding is a positive, somatic experience and an intervention on its own. To help students learn to ground, match your language to their developmental level, and introduce it as the best way to keep physical and emotional balance. The Skills Units in Chapter 4 include activities to practice grounding.

Mindful Awareness

Mindful awareness is a teachable skill with five elements (Siegel, 2007):

1. Observing what is happening without attempting to change what we observe
2. Being nonreactive or coming back easily to emotional equilibrium
3. Describing for ourselves our experience as it is happening
4. Participating by fully giving our attention to what is happening and how we are experiencing this moment
5. Being nonjudgmental by letting judgments go

Brain research has found that although the brain can quickly switch attention from one thing to another, it only attends to one thing at a time (Schumacher et al., 2001). When kids are taught to stop and observe their somatic experiences at the first signals of dysregulation, they are not focusing on what they believe is the source of their distress. They have a moment to think instead of reacting emotionally.

Lantieri (2008) suggested that it is best to first introduce kids to mindful awareness through exercises that mirror daily life, such as mindfully eating or washing hands. Have the students slow their breath and carefully observe themselves in the activity. With practice, mindful awareness can help students become familiar with the indicators of their own emotional states. Once kids experience mindful awareness in a specific activity, expand the practice to situations that are potentially dysregulating. Breath is a good anchor for both grounding and mindful awareness, and it helps kids return to calm attention. Mindful awareness, like any skill, improves with practice. Through mindful awareness, students can intervene on their automatic mental and emotional tendencies. They can step back to simply notice what is going on inside and around them. The Skill Units in Chapter 4 include activities to practice mindful awareness.

Tracking Sensation

Tracking sensation refers to a range of interventions using somatic experience, that is, input from the body. Sensations are physiological happenings in the body that are not associated with thoughts. When our reactions are based only on sensations, we do not stop and think. Sensations give important information about one's current arousal and emotional state. When there is potential for becoming dysregulated, mindful awareness makes it possible to observe sensations and then engage the upper cognitive areas of the brain to make decisions about how to act. The sensations of hyperarousal, for example, can signal a student to slow down and think, making it possible to shift emotional states and master situations that previously only caused trouble.

It is helpful to be familiar with the language of sensations. Pressure, temperature change on the skin, vibrations, warmth, racing heart, jitters, nausea, hunger, muscular tension, tingling or trembling, gut feeling, dizzy feeling, cold or heat, calm or excited, energetic or tired are all examples of sensations. Here are important characteristics of sensations:

- Sensations offer information about our current level of arousal.
- Sensations are not emotions, but they help one to recognize internal emotional states.
- Sensations are often vague and appear to lack a clear precipitating event.
- Sensations are free of interpretations and judgments that can come with emotion.
- Sensations never remain static.
- Sensations are not conscious actions but can be consciously controlled through self-awareness, conscious thought, and self-management.

Working with a student's sensation rather than emotional state is important in helping kids improve self-regulation. A student's strong expression of emotion can be interpreted and the student's attention directed back to his or her somatic experience. For example, instructing a student to put aside the fear, anger, or other strong emotion he or she is beginning to experience and instead notice the sensations offers that student an immediate opportunity to practice. After the student's attention has been directed to the sensation he or she is feeling, wait for a sign that his or her arousal is reduced before going forward. Self-regulation precedes problem solving. The Skill Units in Chapter 4 include activities to practice tracking sensation.

Adults' Calm, Emotionally Regulated State

The most basic intervention adults can use to help students manage their dysregulation and learn to self-regulate is their own emotionally regulated state. Remember, our calm creates calm. A calm emotional state has a positive potential impact on interactions with both students and colleagues. With an individual or a group, an adult's calm emotional state has the potential for calming and reregulating others. As adults working with challenging students, it is helpful for us and our students to use and practice using grounding, mindful awareness, and tracking sensation to remain in a calm state. Include a grounding exercise at the beginning of each day and at any other time it would be beneficial. Use your body awareness to gauge your level of arousal. Dysregulated arousal interferes with the ability to think clearly. Taking the time to reregulate ourselves before interacting with students or others improves our ability to act and to take care of ourselves. We are most helpful when we are energized and calm. Ford and Cloitre (2009) suggested that, while working with a student, we repeatedly ask ourselves this question: "How can I communicate an understanding of this student's state of mind and body that will be meaningful and validating, while moving him or her gradually toward greater integration, self-awareness, and self-control?"

The Importance of Relationship in Improving Self-Regulation

When teachers work toward establishing a safe, positive classroom climate, all students are likely to benefit, including those who have had difficulties in the past. In a review of the research related to school climate and relationships, Christenson and Peterson (2008) described the important role that accepting, cooperative environments play in students' success at school. The authors cite several findings that mention the need for students to have a sense of belonging and not to feel alienated. Research by Domagala-Zysk (2006) concluded that when students are supported by peers and teachers, their grades and overall academic achievement are likely to improve. The author also emphasizes the need for educators to teach them not only academic skills but also how to create and maintain good relationships with others. Birch and Ladd (1998) and Hamre and Pianta (2006) emphasized that positive student–teacher relationships act as a resource for students who are at risk of school failure. The authors also reaffirm that the need for connections between students and educators remains consistent and strong from preschool through 12th grade.

Research and our experience tell us that a relationship with a caring adult can make a significant difference in a student's life. To help students improve their abilities to self-regulate, that adult relationship needs to include several specific qualities: secure attachment, calm interactions, relational attunement, and reflective dialogue. How a student perceives the quality of the student–adult relationship is one of the best predictors of positive behavior change (Bedi, Davis, & Williams, 2005).

Secure Attachment

The student may not have had a relationship based on secure attachment at home, so when we offer a positive, reliable source of calming connection, kids can have a corrective relational experience (Ogden et al., 2006). To offer this corrective relational experience, we work to develop a helping relationship characterized by calm, reliable, emotionally responsive interaction. This kind of relationship improves the student's capacity for self-regulation (Siegel, 2003).

Calm Interactions

To help kids learn to self-regulate, we must be self-regulated and interact with them calmly. First, we must notice our level of arousal and emotions and observe our thoughts and actions and their impact on others. According to Fosha (2003), the arousal, thoughts, emotions, and actions of one individual can affect the internal regulation of another. Known as "interactive affect regulation," it is hypothesized that brain cells called mirror neurons reflect the neural activation patterns of another brain and are involved in interactive affect regulation. From our first contact with the student, we try to establish a helping relationship that students can trust and experience as safe, strong, and calm (van der Kolk, 2007).

Interactive affect regulation can have an impact between adults and kids, as well as between kids and other kids, and between adults and other adults. Kids who are emotionally and behaviorally dysregulated can create chaos and unconsciously induce everyone around them to experience the same emotional dysregulation. To assist students and others who work with them, at times we have to reregulate—calming ourselves in order to offer positive interactive affect regulation. Through our self-regulation we can provide calming experiences, modulating the arousal of those around us (van der Kolk, 2007).

Relational Attunement

When an adult observes a child and attentively responds to his or her signals of comfort or distress, it is referred to as "relational attunement." Much of our interaction with kids is through right-brain to right-brain communication (Schore, 2003). This communication is primarily nonverbal and includes facial expression, tone and volume of voice, body posture, movement, and the instant appraisal of another's facial expression. Through research in interpersonal neurobiology, we know that as the adult learns the child's signals and responds, neural connections are created and the child becomes increasingly able to signal his or her needs and to respond to others (Siegel, 1999). This kind of communication can be used to help a child maintain positive emotions, rapidly metabolize negative affects when they come up, and maximize positive emotional states (Ogden et al., 2006).

Reflective Dialogue

Reflective dialogue is related to interaction and conversation about thoughts, feelings, sensations, perceptions, memories, attitudes, beliefs, and intentions. It is the foundation for the development of mindsight or self-reflection, the capacity to perceive our subjective experience and that of others. When engaging in reflective dialogue with kids, encourage sharing both positive and negative emotions. This kind of activity increases the awareness that emotion can be tolerated internally and helps to deepen kids' capacity for self-observation and self-understanding.

Self-Regulation Skills

In addition to the basic skills of grounding, mindful awareness, and tracking sensation, we incorporate social and emotional learning (SEL) to improve students' abilities to self-regulate. Teaching these self-regulation skills is the process through which kids acquire the knowledge, attitudes, and skills to recognize and manage their emotions, calm themselves when angry, resolve conflicts respectfully, make responsible decisions, handle interpersonal situations effectively, and demonstrate empathy for others. The Collaborative for Academic, Social, and Emotional Learning (CASEL, 2003) has identified five areas of interrelated core social and emotional competencies students need for success: self-awareness, social awareness, self-management, responsible decision making, and relationship skills. This book focuses on specific competencies within these areas that are targeted to improve students' skills in self-regulation. These include the student being able to do the following:

- Describe physical sensations separately from emotions
- Identify and express emotions verbally
- Accept criticism and praise
- Take responsibility for actions
- Initiate a calming strategy after being upset
- Follow directions from adults
- Respond to nonverbal cues
- Demonstrate empathy for others
- Work productively in a group
- Identify consequences before acting
- Manage transitions
- Use resources for obtaining help when getting upset
- Act respectfully to others, regardless of differences
- Respect personal boundaries, rights, and property of others
- Negotiate with others when there is disagreement

The Skill Units in Chapter 4 include a wide variety of suggestions and lessons for developing and reinforcing these skills.

Challenging students with severe behavioral difficulties cause serious concern among educators, parents, and advocates. Concerns exist that the excessive and untrained use of restraint and seclusion of students is dangerous, overly restrictive, and detrimental to the educational process. The literature now attributes many of the behaviors of concern in schools to difficulties with self-regulation. Additionally, the literature demonstrates that it is possible to teach students skills to increase their capacity for self-regulation and avoid the serious behaviors that come about from behavioral dysregulation. The next chapter describes a model for reducing the use of restraint and seclusion when addressing serious behavioral difficulties.

Chapter 3
A Model for Positive Alternatives to Restraint and Seclusion

We make use of the solution-focused approach while taking into account the problems that students with self-regulation difficulties present in schools. With the solution-focused approach, we are advocating a shift in thinking from "What's wrong?" to "How do we want things to be?" and "What would improvement look like?" Our goals are to identify and utilize the student's strengths and to create explicit behavioral objectives for improvement.

Referral

The first step in the intervention process is often the initial referral of the student for consideration. When we receive a referral about a student who is having trouble with self-regulation, the referring source often knows what is wrong and has ideas about how to fix the problem, but he or she often has difficulty explaining the *desired* behaviors. Frequently, the referrer discusses *why* the student is behaving a certain way or repeats what the student is doing wrong. The task for those charged with intervening with the student is to translate this dialogue about the problem into potential solutions or goals by asking the referring source to describe signs of a successful improvement or outcome in concrete, behavioral, and measurable ways. The Referral Discussion Guide, shown in Appendix 3.A, includes information for getting a behavioral description of the problem, information about the circumstances in which the problem occurs, and descriptions of improvement behaviors.

Meetings and Conferences

Meetings and conferences are excellent settings for using solution-focused talk to arrive at a goal and a plan for improving a student's ability to self-regulate. The principles that guide solution-focused work facilitate working successfully with students, parents, teachers, and other school personnel. The guidelines follow, with examples of possible statements.

- Accept, acknowledge, and accommodate the person's view of what has been happening.
    - *Sounds like Todd's meltdowns have been a disaster for your class.*
    - *It must have been tough trying to manage Todd's behavior and teach the rest of the class. How have you been able to manage so far?*
- Solicit action talk—a behavioral description—with follow-up questions to their problem statements.
    - *What do you see that tells you Todd is having a meltdown?*
    - *What would I notice that would tell me Todd is having a really bad day?*
- Listen for exceptions to the problem.
    - *Tell me about a time when Todd was able to avoid a meltdown or had a less severe reaction.*
    - *What was happening that day? What seemed different?*
- Solicit their idea of a goal for improvement.
    - *What can you see happening that would be an improvement, if even a little?*

- *Of all the troublesome behaviors you're seeing, with which one would a little improvement make the most difference?*
- Compliment their effective actions or thoughts.
  - *That's unbelievable—you could remain calm under those circumstances. Most people would have lost it, but you didn't. How were you able to do that?*
  - *I appreciate the way you are supporting my work with (student's name) by encouraging the practice of grounding in your classroom.*

The following are some advantages to taking the solution-focused approach with referring parties:

- We can acknowledge all they have been doing already.
- We can support them in continuing to work with a difficult situation.
- We change the viewing (their perspective) and the doing (the actions) so they can envision improved behavior and what that looks like for the kid.
- We can use their behavioral description to give us a much better idea of the problem and the solution.
- We are able to shift their focus to instances when the problem is not quite so bad, what they are doing when the problem is occurring, and what difference this will make in their interactions with the kid.

Establishing Goals

The process of developing goals is often overlooked in the push for quick solutions. This is especially true when the referring persons already have a definite idea of a goal. In this model, we work to identify the kid's goal for change, and the goal we arrive at should encompass the kid's ideas for a solution. Developing goals in collaboration with kids, parents, and teachers can be challenging. However, it is well worth the effort, because goals keep our work on track and provide clear criteria for evaluating its effectiveness. Solution-focused goals are significant, specific, small, self-manageable, and define a place to start (Murphy, 2008).

Description of the Materials, and Directions for Use

Positive Alternatives to Restraint and Seclusion for Aggressive Kids includes a Referral Discussion Guide, a Student Intervention Plan, Reproducible Tools, and Skill Units. We will discuss each here.

Referral Discussion Guide

Located in Appendix 3.A, this guide facilitates specific information-gathering that is useful in planning. Teachers, administrators, and others who know the student well can submit this request.

Student Intervention Plan

This plan, available in a print version in Appendix 3.A and as a modifiable form on the enclosed CD, is a thorough, detailed, easy-to-use form that student intervention teams, response to intervention (RtI) teams, discipline committees, and others can use when intervening with aggressive students. The form is useful as a method for

- identifying students for intervention,
- describing students' behaviors,
- designing and planning a specific intervention plan, and
- documenting interventions and progress.

The plan can be printed individually from the CD. To preserve the plan template, follow these steps:

- Perform a Save As with the student's name or ID number.
- Enter the data by typing in the spaces.
- Select the boxes by typing an "X" in the box.
- Save and Print the plan.

The Student Intervention Plan has five main components:

Section I: Reason(s) for Intervention

Section I is a checklist that educators can use as a referral tool for deciding which students need intensive behavioral interventions. There is limited research on which behaviors precipitate the use of restraint and seclusion. A review of the literature and interviews with administrators, teachers, behavior specialists, counselors, and others were used to assist in the construction of this checklist.

In addition to the checklist, educators are urged to use other diagnostic and screening instruments, data reviews, and observations in order to get a comprehensive picture of a student's pattern of behavior.

Student Intervention Plan

First Name: Ryan
Last Name: Johnson
ID #: 567892
Campus: Shore Middle School/ 7th grade
Team Leader: B. Donnelly
Date: Nov. 5

SECTION I: REASON(S) FOR INTERVENTION

Check all that apply.

- [X] Initiates physical fights with others
- [ ] Has brought a weapon to school that can cause serious physical harm to others
- [X] Bullies, threatens, or frightens others
- [X] Is physically aggressive
- [X] Destroys or takes others' property
- [X] Has tantrums
- [X] Is verbally aggressive
- [ ] Argues with adults
- [X] Defies or refuses to comply with adult's requests or directions
- [ ] Uses profane or obscene language
- [ ] Encourages misbehavior of others in the classroom
- [ ] Refuses to comply with school and/or classroom rules and procedures
- [ ] Intentionally annoys or teases others
- [ ] Leaves seat or work area without permission
- [ ] Interrupts instruction by making inappropriate comments

Section II: Discipline Data

Section II of the Student Intervention Plan can be used to document prior actions taken related to extreme behaviors. Because the plan is designed for use with students whose behaviors are very severe, documenting prior actions taken is essential. Team members should indicate how often the student had been subject to restraint, seclusion, office referrals, detentions or in-school suspensions, out-of-school suspensions, arrests or other incidents involving law-enforcement officials, and other pertinent actions. As a general rule, the more often a student has engaged in aggressive behavior, the more often he or she will have faced serious consequences. However, there is not always a one-to-one relationship between incidents and consequences, so the team should gather all relevant information when considering interventions for a student.

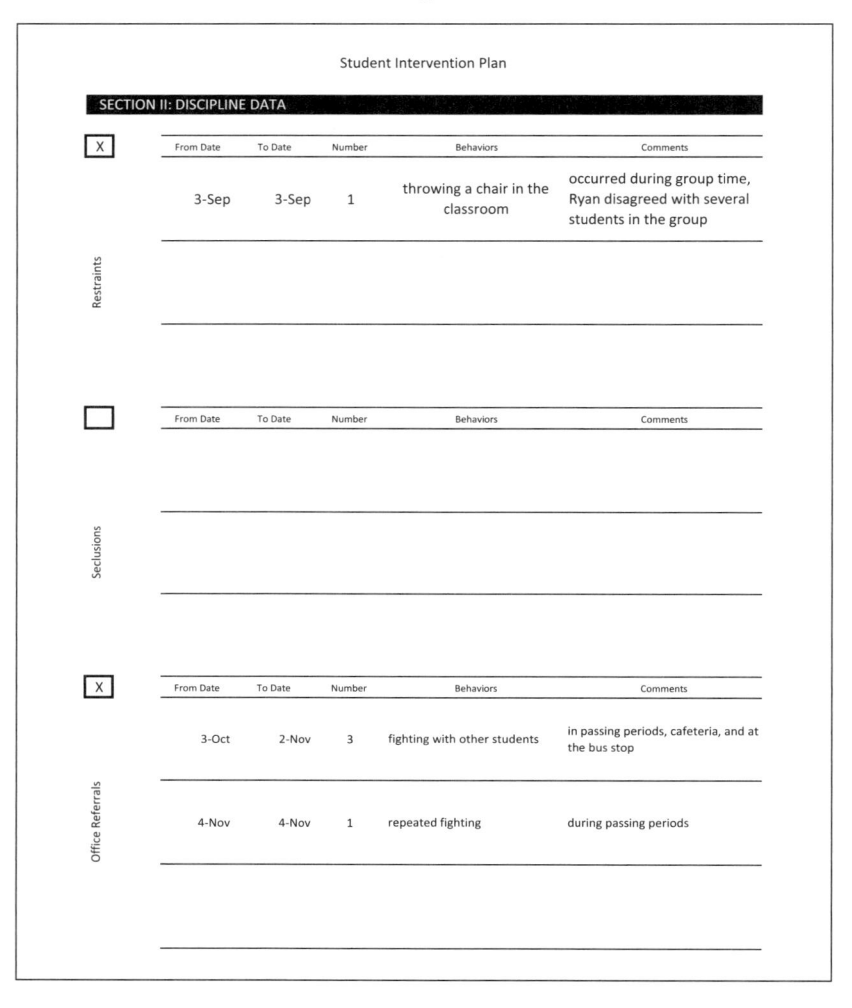

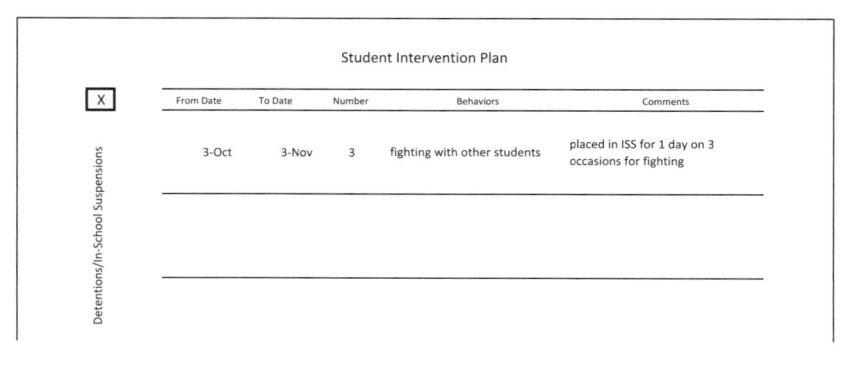

Student Intervention Plan

SECTION II: DISCIPLINE DATA

Restraints [X]

From Date	To Date	Number	Behaviors	Comments
3-Sep	3-Sep	1	throwing a chair in the classroom	occurred during group time, Ryan disagreed with several students in the group

Seclusions [ ]

From Date	To Date	Number	Behaviors	Comments

Office Referrals [X]

From Date	To Date	Number	Behaviors	Comments
3-Oct	2-Nov	3	fighting with other students	in passing periods, cafeteria, and at the bus stop
4-Nov	4-Nov	1	repeated fighting	during passing periods

Student Intervention Plan

Detentions/In-School Suspensions [X]

From Date	To Date	Number	Behaviors	Comments
3-Oct	3-Nov	3	fighting with other students	placed in ISS for 1 day on 3 occasions for fighting

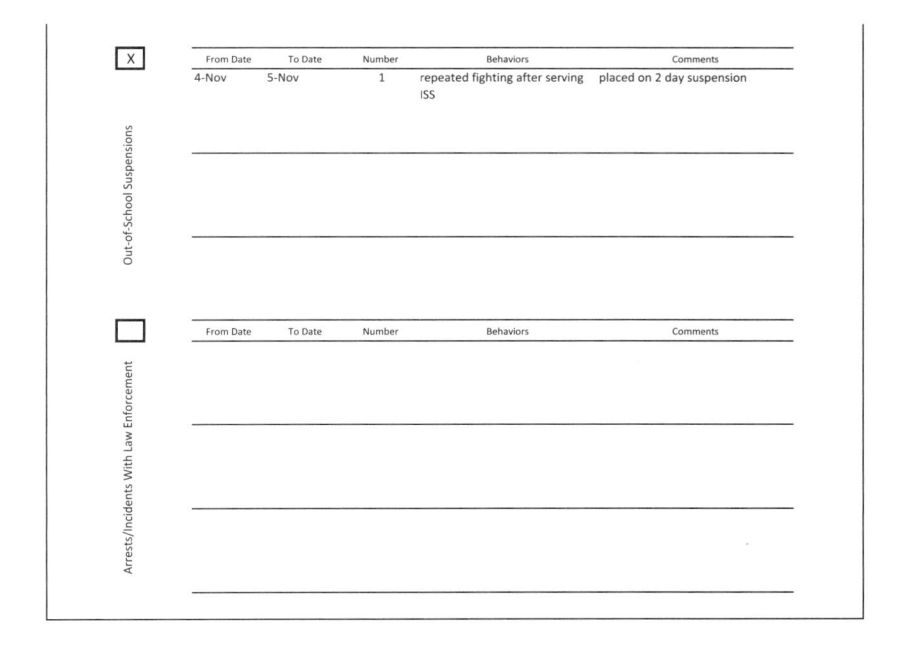

	From Date	To Date	Number	Behaviors	Comments
X (Out-of-School Suspensions)	4-Nov	5-Nov	1	repeated fighting after serving ISS	placed on 2 day suspension

	From Date	To Date	Number	Behaviors	Comments
☐ (Arrests/Incidents With Law Enforcement)					

Section III: Self-Regulation Skills Checklist

Section III of the form allows educators to rate the student's competencies on 15 important self-regulation skills. The rating of the student can be completed using Section III or the Referral Discussion Guide (see Appendix 3.A), which both refer to the same list of essential competencies. These ratings can be repeated for comparison over time. Educators can use the initial information in Section III as a baseline and then use it again to monitor progress after interventions have begun. Allowing a period of 4 to 6 weeks between ratings will provide time for the student to make behavioral changes, but, for many students, the changes will require significantly longer periods of time.

Student Intervention Plan

SECTION III: SELF-REGULATION SKILLS CHECKLIST

Rate the skills: 0 = never, 1 = sometimes, 2 = often, 3 = always

		Date	10-Nov		
		Rater	G. Thomas		
1	Describes physical sensations separately from emotions.		2		
2	Expresses emotions verbally.		2		
3	Accepts criticism and praise.		1		
4	Takes responsibility for actions.		0		
5	Initiates a calming strategy after being upset.		0		
6	Follows directions from adults.		0		
7	Responds to nonverbal cues.		1		
8	Demonstrates empathy for others.		1		
9	Works productively in a group.		1		
10	Identifies consequences before acting.		1		
11	Manages transitions.		1		
12	Uses resources for obtaining help when getting upset.		0		
13	Attends to task, ignores distractions.		1		
14	Respects personal boundaries, rights, and property of others.		1		
15	Negotiates with others when there is disagreement.		1		

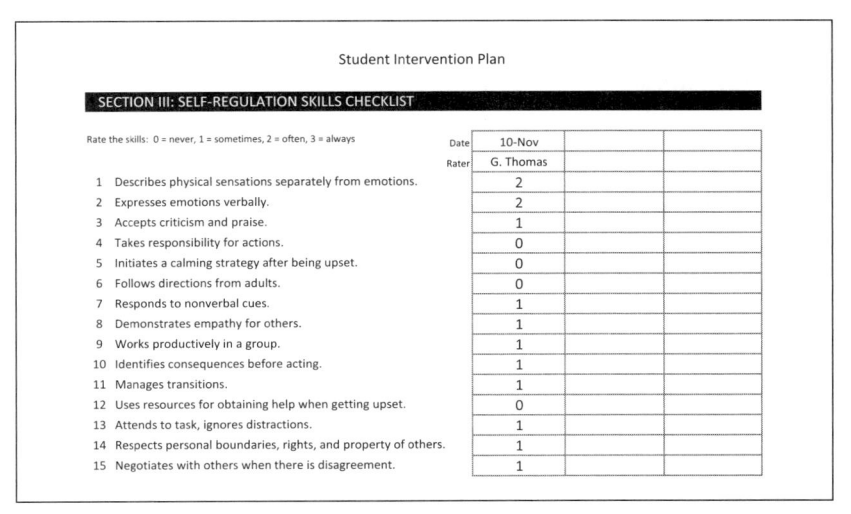

Section IV: Self-Regulation Skills Addressed in This Intervention Plan

Section IV is critical, because it targets specific positive skills and behaviors the student should master for his or her behavior to improve. It is best to target a limited number of self-regulation skills (e.g., 1–3). Trying to intervene on more than three skills is likely to dilute the power of the interventions and may cause adults to become frustrated or overwhelmed. Focusing only on the key skills related to a student's needs, as identified in Section III, is more likely to be effective. For campus intervention, prereferral, or RtI teams, targeting positive skills is essential so that data can be collected and reviewed on the student's progress in mastering those skills. (Refer to Appendix 3.B for a description of and a number of useful forms that can be used for progress monitoring.) The monitoring will be most effective when all educators involved in the process are clear about which skills are targeted for improvement.

The skills identified in Section IV are also important for planning purposes. After first identifying key skills for improvement, school personnel can then select interventions for implementation. The interventions are designed to teach specific skills, and, while there may be some overlap (i.e., an intervention may help a student master more than one skill), it is best to focus on interventions that match the skills each student needs to learn.

SECTION IV: SELF-REGULATION SKILLS ADDRESSED IN THIS INTERVENTION PLAN

Select the top 3 priorities for intervention.

- [ ] Describes physical sensations separately from emotions.
- [ ] Expresses emotions verbally.
- [ ] Accepts criticism and praise.
- [ ] Takes responsibility for actions.
- [1] Initiates a calming strategy after being upset.
- [2] Follows directions from adults.
- [ ] Responds to nonverbal cues.
- [ ] Demonstrates empathy for others.
- [ ] Works productively in a group.
- [ ] Identifies consequences before acting.
- [ ] Manages transitions.
- [3] Uses resources for obtaining help when getting upset.
- [ ] Attends to task, ignores distractions.
- [ ] Respects personal boundaries, rights, and property of others.
- [ ] Negotiates with others when there is disagreement.

Section V: Intervention Timeline and Personnel Responsible

Section V allows teachers, counselors, administrators, behavior specialists and others, who usually work as a team, to select and describe the interventions that match the student's needs and are acceptable to everyone responsible for their implementation. To complete this section of the Student Intervention Plan, educators should refer to the Skill Units in Chapter 4 that correspond to the selected self-regulation skills. In Chapter 3, the Close Monitoring of Behavior section in Appendix 3.B offers a number of interventions for monitoring student behavior.

Before completing Section V of the Student Intervention Plan, team members should read and review the interventions included in the Skill Units, 1 through 15. Interventions should match the student's needs, age, style of interaction, and current educational placement. Not all interventions will work with all students, and not all interventions will match all adults' communication and interaction skills (e.g., teachers may be more competent in some areas whereas counselors may be more skilled in others). When more than one adult is responsible for implementing an intervention, everyone must agree on who will take the lead and how information will be shared. Completing this section of the form will provide documentation, so that when the team meets to consider the student's progress, it will be clear who is responsible for implementation. Educators involved in the meeting and implementing the student's plan should record the date that interventions will begin, the date that progress will be monitored, and the names and titles of participants. This information is especially important when considering interventions for students with disabilities and should be coordinated and integrated into the student's Behavioral Intervention Plan (BIP), if applicable.

Student Intervention Plan

SECTION V: INTERVENTION TIMELINE AND PERSONNEL RESPONSIBLE

Intervention	Person Responsible	Beginning Date	Progress Review Date	Progress Review Date
Use Contract Ideas form (p. 65) to generate common goals for intervention and what improvements will look like.	Counselor, Lead Teacher, Assistant Principal	7-Nov	7-Jan	7-Mar
Use Goal Setting form (p. 62) with Ryan to have him state his goals, ways to reach the goals and what improvement will look like.	Counselor	7-Nov	7-Jan	7-Mar
Use Self-Regulation Progress form (p. 52) to help Ryan rate his progress on demonstrating self-regulation skills.	Counselor and teachers	7-Nov	7-Jan	7-Mar
Use Getting Calm Feels Great (p. 112) to help Ryan chart his progress.	Counselor and teachers	7-Nov	7-Jan	7-Mar
Use Skill Unit 6	Teachers	7-Dec	7-Feb	7-Apr
Skill Unit 6 activity Say OK, Take a Ticket	Teachers	7-Jan	7-Feb	7-Mar
Skill Unit 6 activity After & Before	Teachers	7-Jan	7-Feb	7-Mar
Hold conference with Ryan and his parents to coordinate the approach with home and plan for communication.	Counselor, Lead Teacher	7-Nov	7-Feb	7-Apr

Additional Information

Typical participants involved in planning for aggressive students include a teacher, counselor, administrator, behavior specialist, psychologist, and social worker. At additional meetings to review progress and possibly change the student's plan, participants may be different from the original meeting, so it is important to know who was involved in the initial consideration and plan development.

Reproducible Tools

Positive Alternatives to Restraint and Seclusion for Aggressive Kids contains reproducible tools, which include interventions for students whose behaviors are likely to hurt others or themselves.

The Close Monitoring of Behavior section in Appendix 3.B contains a variety of forms that can be used to record a student's behaviors. These forms are easy to use, but it is important to summarize the data regularly (e.g., weekly at first, then every 2 to 3 weeks) so that the student's progress can be evaluated. With this information, the team can determine whether the current interventions are having the desired impact and, if not, to revise or discontinue them and try another intervention from the manual.

The reproducible materials on the CD are the same as those printed in the manual and are compatible with most computers.

The manual includes a CD containing an electronic version of the Student Intervention Plan and all reproducible forms and activities. The interventions contained in the manual are easy to understand and can be implemented by counselors, teachers, behavior specialists, administrators, and others. Most of the interventions are designed to be used regularly, over time. Because the students who require these interventions have very serious behaviors, it is unlikely that their patterns of interactions in school and elsewhere will change quickly. Consistent follow-through by adults will be needed. In addition, educators should expect that, even if the interventions are implemented faithfully, a student's pattern of behavior change may not be consistent. The student may show improvement for a time, and then regress. Such irregular behavior patterns are common among students with serious emotional and behavioral disorders as well as among students who have autism spectrum disorders and other disabilities. Teachers and others should expect students to demonstrate some improvement in their self-regulation skills, experience setbacks, and then show additional improvement.

Skill Units

Each Skill Unit in Chapter 4 is organized for easy use. First we provide background research-based information regarding the skill. This section includes quick tips, activities, and strategies for use with the student. In the targeted skill that follows the introduction, the important components of each idea are explained and include the following:

- target skill or skills addressed by the intervention
- materials needed to implement the idea
- explanation of the skills
- rationale for the intervention
- procedures for implementing the intervention
- special circumstances or adaptations that can be used when implementing the intervention

After ensuring that everyone who will be intervening understands the intervention, duplicate the related materials. These supplementary materials include forms, contracts, visuals, and other tools that will enhance the intervention and assist with documentation. The related materials are also included as PDFs on the CD.

All professionals who implement the interventions contained this manual should continue implementation for a reasonable period of time. For young students, this could be 4 to 6 weeks; for older students, 6 to 10 weeks. Remember that many students' patterns of aggressive behavior are well-established and reinforced by many variables. Involving the student throughout the process to incorporate his or her goals for behavior improvement will increase the likelihood of positive change (Murphy, 2008). It is critical to take a positive attitude, expect the best, and evaluate progress regularly. When students need to make more progress, use the manual as a resource for additional interventions. Team members can discontinue an intervention and begin another as necessary.

Appendix 3.A

- **Referral Discussion Guide**

- **Student Intervention Plan**

Referral Discussion Guide

Student: _____ Campus: _____

Date: _____ Teacher: _____

Describe the behavior of concern with this student:

Describe the circumstances surrounding this behavior:

Before	
During	
After	
Setting	
Who is there?	

What will this student do differently when there is resolution of the problem(s)?

What would be evidence of a solid first step towards that goal?

Describe the times when parts of the goal have already been achieved.

How would you account for the student's progress toward the goal at those times?

Put a check in the column that indicates the student's ability to do the following:

	Never	Sometimes	Often	Almost Always
Describes physical sensations separately from emotions.				
Expresses emotions verbally.				
Accepts criticism and praise.				
Takes responsibility for actions.				
Initiates a calming strategy after being upset.				
Follows directions from adults.				
Responds to nonverbal cues.				
Demonstrates empathy for others.				
Works productively in a group.				
Identifies consequences before acting.				
Manages transitions.				
Uses resources for obtaining help when getting upset.				
Attends to task, ignores distractions.				
Respects personal boundaries, rights, and property of others.				
Negotiates with others when there is disagreement.				

© 2012 by PRO-ED, Inc.   #13936

Student Intervention Plan

First Name _____   Campus _____
Last Name _____   Team Leader _____
ID # _____   Date _____

SECTION I: REASON(S) FOR INTERVENTION

Check all that apply.

- [ ] Initiates physical fights with others
- [ ] Has brought a weapon to school that can cause serious physical harm to others
- [ ] Bullies, threatens, or frightens others
- [ ] Is physically aggressive
- [ ] Destroys or takes others' property
- [ ] Has tantrums
- [ ] Is verbally aggressive
- [ ] Argues with adults
- [ ] Defies or refuses to comply with adult's requests or directions
- [ ] Uses profane or obscene language
- [ ] Encourages misbehavior of others in the classroom
- [ ] Refuses to comply with school and/or classroom rules and procedures
- [ ] Intentionally annoys or teases others
- [ ] Leaves seat or work area without permission
- [ ] Interrupts instruction by making inappropriate comments

© 2012 by PRO-ED, Inc.   # 13936 Positive Alternatives to Restraint and Seclusion

Student Intervention Plan

SECTION II: DISCIPLINE DATA

☐ **Restraints**

From Date	To Date	Number	Behaviors	Comments

☐ **Seclusions**

From Date	To Date	Number	Behaviors	Comments

☐ **Office Referrals**

From Date	To Date	Number	Behaviors	Comments

Student Intervention Plan

☐ | From Date | To Date | Number | Behaviors | Comments

Detentions/In-School Suspensions

☐ | From Date | To Date | Number | Behaviors | Comments

Out-of-School Suspensions

☐ | From Date | To Date | Number | Behaviors | Comments

Arrests/Incidents With Law Enforcement

Student Intervention Plan

SECTION III: SELF-REGULATION SKILLS CHECKLIST

Rate the skills: 0 = never, 1 = sometimes, 2 = often, 3 = always

	Date			
	Rater			
1	Describes physical sensations separately from emotions.			
2	Expresses emotions verbally.			
3	Accepts criticism and praise.			
4	Takes responsibility for actions.			
5	Initiates a calming strategy after being upset.			
6	Follows directions from adults.			
7	Responds to nonverbal cues.			
8	Demonstrates empathy for others.			
9	Works productively in a group.			
10	Identifies consequences before acting.			
11	Manages transitions.			
12	Uses resources for obtaining help when getting upset.			
13	Attends to task, ignores distractions.			
14	Respects personal boundaries, rights, and property of others.			
15	Negotiates with others when there is disagreement.			

SECTION IV: SELF-REGULATION SKILLS ADDRESSED IN THIS INTERVENTION PLAN

Select the top 3 priorities for intervention.

- ☐ Describes physical sensations separately from emotions.
- ☐ Expresses emotions verbally.
- ☐ Accepts criticism and praise.
- ☐ Takes responsibility for actions.
- ☐ Initiates a calming strategy after being upset.
- ☐ Follows directions from adults.
- ☐ Responds to nonverbal cues.
- ☐ Demonstrates empathy for others.
- ☐ Works productively in a group.
- ☐ Identifies consequences before acting.
- ☐ Manages transitions.
- ☐ Uses resources for obtaining help when getting upset.
- ☐ Attends to task, ignores distractions.
- ☐ Respects personal boundaries, rights, and property of others.
- ☐ Negotiates with others when there is disagreement.

© 2012 by PRO-ED, Inc.   # 13936 Positive Alternatives to Restraint and Seclusion

Student Intervention Plan

SECTION V: INTERVENTION TIMELINE AND PERSONNEL RESPONSIBLE

Intervention	Person Responsible	Beginning Date	Progress Review Date	Progress Review Date

Additional Information

Appendix 3.B: Close Monitoring of Behavior

All students who have demonstrated behavior problems should be monitored throughout the school day. Students whose behavior patterns have included serious acting-out and aggression should be monitored very closely by all adults, in all school settings, all day long. In many cases, monitoring forms or systems can also be effectively linked to systems of positive reinforcement of the students' appropriate behavior. Research (Colvin, Sugai, Good, & Lee, 1997; Lewis, Sugai, & Colvin, 2000) supports close monitoring of serious behaviors for several reasons:

1. When adults frequently and regularly monitor behavior, misbehavior and behavior improvements can be identified early. Most students' misbehavior follows a pattern, and intervening early, while the problems are minor or infrequent, can prevent more serious or more frequent misbehavior. Such intervention is helpful in preventing the need for physical intervention.
2. After adults have monitored students' behavior over time, it is possible to identify triggers or antecedents that typically lead to student misbehavior. This allows intervention even *before* the behavior has begun. Such intervention decreases the need for after-the-fact responses, because interventions can be focused on preventive actions. It is just as important to notice and congratulate students when their positive behaviors are evident. Compliment with specific descriptions, and attribute success to students' efforts.
3. Close monitoring provides useful information about whether current interventions are working. By summarizing and reviewing the data provided by close monitoring, administrators, teachers, counselors, and others can make informed judgments regarding whether to initiate, continue, modify, or discontinue specific interventions.
4. Behavior-monitoring information can be very helpful when communicating with students' parents or guardians. Sometimes, parents do not have a clear understanding of what is expected of their child in school. Nor do they always have a realistic view of how their children behave when they are not at home. Reliable information that can be used in parent–teacher conferences and in IEP meetings is often very helpful.
5. Close monitoring can also point out problems within the school environment. Often, a student's behavior may be a reaction to a specific stressor, such as a difficult class; a teacher whose personality clashes with that of the student; or a large, busy setting (like a cafeteria) that does not provide enough structure for some students. Decisions about changes in schedules and levels of support for students should be based on current, reliable information, like that provided through close monitoring.
6. Finally, monitoring students' behavior is an essential component of a thorough Functional Behavior Assessment (FBA). When conducting an FBA and writing a Behavioral Intervention Plan, the data gathered through daily or even hourly behavior monitoring can be critical.

There are several important considerations for monitoring student behavior:

- It is critical that the teachers, counselors, behavior specialists, instructional assistants, or others who are monitoring student behavior are comfortable with the tools they are asked to use. Forms and systems that are overly time-consuming, complicated, or irrelevant will not be used with fidelity and are unlikely to be successful.
- Systems for monitoring a student's behavior must be designed after careful consideration of the student's age, disability status, level of cognitive functioning, and past experience. This is especially true to those monitoring strategies that are linked to positive reinforcement.
- Just completing a daily or weekly monitoring form usually will not be enough to change behavior by itself. Often, students need to self-monitor or to participate in a system of positive reinforcement that links their behavior to privileges or tangible rewards in order for the monitoring to have an impact. In addition, thoughtful long-term interventions, such as those provided in this manual, will likely be necessary.
- For monitoring efforts to really pay off, data must be summarized, reviewed, discussed and changes must be made to programming, when necessary. When a program that includes monitoring begins, set timelines for consideration of the information that will be gathered.

The following pages include tools for monitoring student behavior. The focus of the tools, like the focus of these materials, is on students whose behaviors are very serious, including acting-out behaviors and aggression. These forms can also be found as PDFs on the accompanying CD.

- **Behavior Tracker for Young Students**, page 31
- **Positive Behavior in Pictures**, page 33
- **Daily Behavior Chart**, page 35
- **Daily Progress in Self-Control**, page 38
- **Weekly Monitoring**, page 40
- **Earn It/Lose It**, page 42
- **Self-Monitoring Tool**, page 45
- **Self-Regulation Progress**, page 48
- **To Reach My Goal**, page 51
- **Behavior Improvement Drawings**, page 54
- **Check Off My Progress!**, page 57
- **Goal Setting**, page 59
- **Contract Ideas**, page 62
- **Progress Toward Goal**, page 65
- **Notice the Pattern**, page 67

Behavior Tracker for Young Students

The Behavior Tracker for Young Students visually represents a specific behavior and a student's daily schedule. The use of visuals makes it possible to clearly communicate the behavior being tracked to young children who are not yet able to read. In addition, the form allows for positive reinforcement when the student demonstrates the desired behavior. After reviewing progress with the student at the end of the day, teachers, counselors, or others should keep track of how many positives the student earned for the day. This will allow for evaluation of overall progress.

Directions

To complete the *Behavior Tracker for Young Students*, first complete a visual representation of the target behavior. Photographs, icons, or picture symbols are all appropriate and useful when completing this form. Discuss with the student his or her goal and what positive rewards he or she would like to earn when behavior is appropriate. Next, use visuals to represent the student's schedule in the first column of the form. After each class or activity, review the student's behavior with him or her and circle to indicate positive performance (happy face) or inappropriate behaviors (sad face). Make sure the student participates in the discussion to process how well he or she did and how to improve.

Note. This idea is adapted from *Practical Ideas That Really Work for Students with Disruptive, Defiant, or Difficult Behaviors: Preschool Through Grade 4* (2nd ed., p. 162), by K. McConnell, G. R. Ryser, and J. R. Patton, 2010, Austin, TX: PRO-ED. Copyright 2010 by PRO-ED, Inc. Reprinted with permission.

	☺
	☹
	☺
	☹
	☺
	☹
	☺
	☹

You need _____ ☺

You earned _____ ☺

You earned your choice of

| | or | |

	☺
	☹
	☺
	☹
	☺
	☹
	☺
	☹

You need _____ ☺

You earned _____ ☺

You earned your choice of

| | or | |

© 2012 by PRO-ED, Inc.   #13936

Positive Behavior in Pictures

This form is effective with young students who need visual representations of behaviors and short intervals for monitoring. To use a half or a whole day, reduce the size of the form, and put several intervals on a page. The form also functions as a reminder for positive reinforcement.

Directions

Choose two basic target behaviors and two reinforcers. Indicate the goals to the student by using pictures or symbols that represent the behaviors and reinforcers. Fill in the time intervals, circle the faces, and reinforce if the behavior has been on target. As you circle a smiley face, don't forget to praise the student. This form will work best if the student selects the reinforcers and reviews the behavior each morning; then, each afternoon, review progress with the student. Track totals and a percentage of positive behaviors to measure progress.

Note. This idea is adapted from *Practical Ideas That Really Work for Students with Autism Sprectrum Disorders: Preschool Through Grade 4* (2nd ed., p. 158), by K. McConnell and G. R. Ryser, 2007, Austin, TX: PRO-ED. Copyright 2007 by PRO-ED, Inc. Reprinted with permission.

Positive Behavior In Pictures

Name _____   Date _____

Time Intervals

Behaviors	___ to ___	Reinforcer	___ to ___	Reinforcer	___ to ___	Reinforcer	___ to ___	Reinforcer
	:) :(		:) :(		:) :(		:) :(	
	:) :(		:) :(		:) :(		:) :(	

Total :) :)
Percent

Total :)

© 2012 by PRO-ED, Inc.   #13936

Daily Behavior Chart

Use the Daily Behavior Chart for monitoring one to three behaviors during each time interval of the school day (e.g., class or subject period). The chart can be used for a whole school day or a half day, depending on the schedule. The key behaviors on the chart should reflect specific concerns for students who are acting out or aggressive. Describe the presence of an appropriate behavior rather than the stopping of an inappropriate behavior.

Directions

To complete the chart, circle one of the indicators that describes the student's behavior as Not Okay, Okay, or Great at the end of each class period:

Not Okay ☹

Okay 😐

Great 🙂

The chart can be used with younger students as well because of the easily understood smiley-face icons. At the end of each day, discuss and summarize the student's performance with the student. Based on a summary of the daily charts, compute a weekly and monthly percentage of acceptable performance.

Daily Behavior Chart

Student Name _____ Date _____

Please indicate how well the student performed on the target behavior by circling one of the descriptors.

Class or Time Period	First Behavior:	Second Behavior:	Third Behavior:	Adult's Initials and Comments:
	Not Okay ☹ Okay 😐 Great 🙂	Not Okay ☹ Okay 😐 Great 🙂	Not Okay ☹ Okay 😐 Great 🙂	
	Not Okay ☹ Okay 😐 Great 🙂	Not Okay ☹ Okay 😐 Great 🙂	Not Okay ☹ Okay 😐 Great 🙂	
	Not Okay ☹ Okay 😐 Great 🙂	Not Okay ☹ Okay 😐 Great 🙂	Not Okay ☹ Okay 😐 Great 🙂	
	Not Okay ☹ Okay 😐 Great 🙂	Not Okay ☹ Okay 😐 Great 🙂	Not Okay ☹ Okay 😐 Great 🙂	
	Not Okay ☹ Okay 😐 Great 🙂	Not Okay ☹ Okay 😐 Great 🙂	Not Okay ☹ Okay 😐 Great 🙂	
	Not Okay ☹ Okay 😐 Great 🙂	Not Okay ☹ Okay 😐 Great 🙂	Not Okay ☹ Okay 😐 Great 🙂	
	Total Okay: _____ Total Great: _____	Total Okay: _____ Total Great: _____	Total Okay: _____ Total Great: _____	% Okay: _____ % Great: _____

The next date for a review of the Daily Behavior Chart is: _____.

Daily Behavior Chart (Example)

Student Name __Carlos Herrera__ Date __January 4, 2012__

Please indicate how well the student performed on the target behavior by circling one of the descriptors.

Class or Time Period	First Behavior:	Second Behavior:	Third Behavior:	Adult's Initials and Comments:
Breakfast	Not Okay ☹ Okay 😐 Great 🙂 (circled)	Not Okay ☹ Okay 😐 Great 🙂	Not Okay ☹ Okay 😐 Great 🙂	C.J. Good job waiting for turn.
Reading/ELA	Not Okay ☹ Okay 😐 Great 🙂	Not Okay ☹ Okay 😐 Great 🙂	Not Okay ☹ Okay 😐 Great 🙂	
Math	Not Okay ☹ Okay 😐 Great 🙂	Not Okay ☹ Okay 😐 Great 🙂	Not Okay ☹ Okay 😐 Great 🙂	
Social Studies/Science	Not Okay ☹ Okay 😐 Great 🙂	Not Okay ☹ Okay 😐 Great 🙂	Not Okay ☹ Okay 😐 Great 🙂	
Lunch	Not Okay ☹ Okay 😐 Great 🙂	Not Okay ☹ Okay 😐 Great 🙂	Not Okay ☹ Okay 😐 Great 🙂	
PE/Fine Arts	Not Okay ☹ Okay 😐 Great 🙂	Not Okay ☹ Okay 😐 Great 🙂	Not Okay ☹ Okay 😐 Great 🙂	
	Total Okay: ____ Total Great: ____	Total Okay: ____ Total Great: ____	Total Okay: ____ Total Great: ____	% Okay: ____ % Great: ____

The next date for a review of the Daily Behavior Chart is: _____.

Daily Progress in Self-Control

This form tracks three specific behaviors and rates a student's level of self-control throughout a school day.

Directions

Check the appropriate box to indicate whether the student was on time, had materials, completed his or her work, and demonstrated self-control. To rate the student's behavior as excellent, fair, or poor, use the key at the bottom of the chart, and initial the Teacher's Initials box. Make sure that a case manager reviews and reinforces the student at the end of the day. Send this form home daily with the student so that the parent can provide a reinforcer for appropriate behavior.

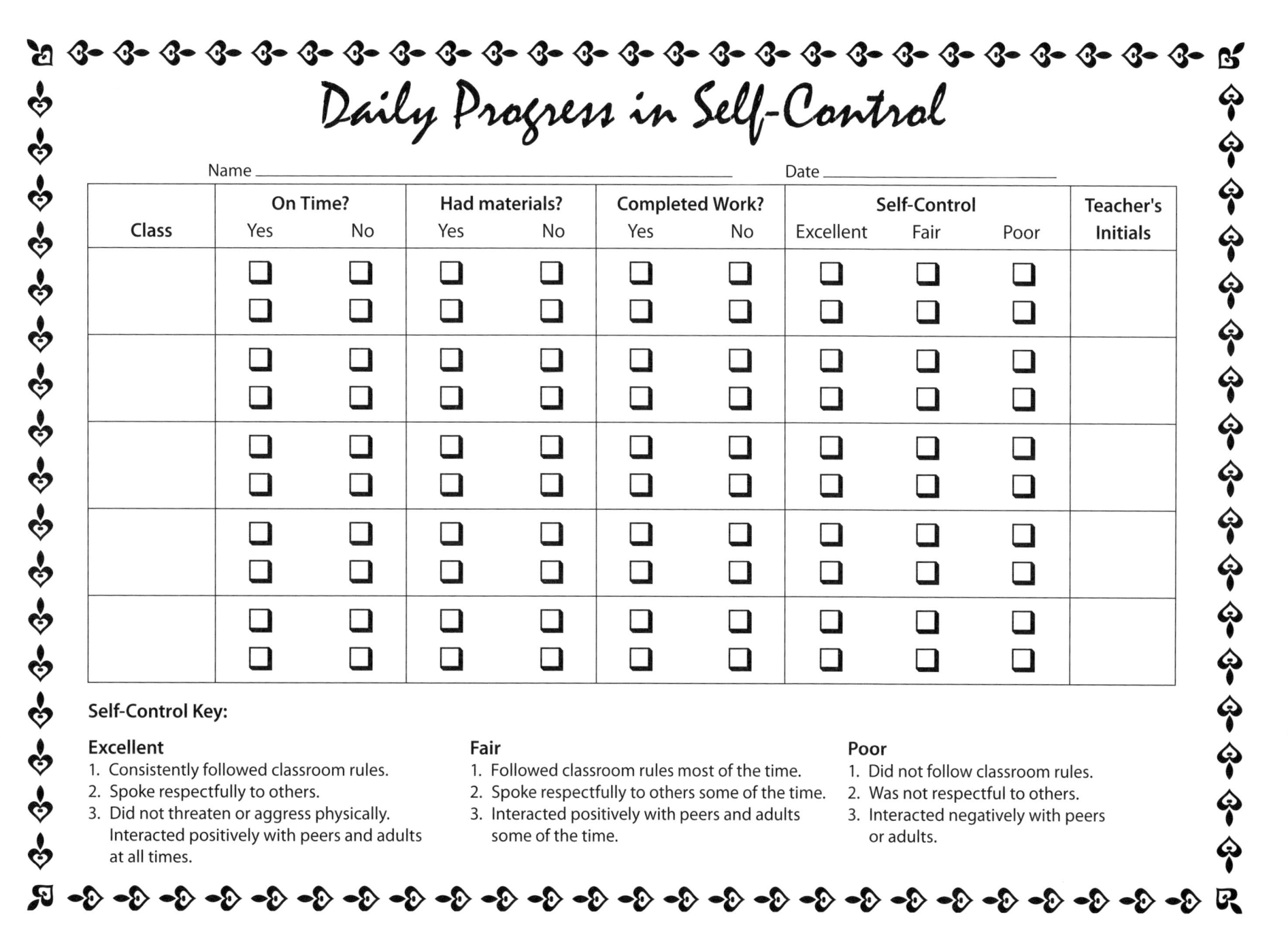

Daily Progress in Self-Control

Name _____ Date _____

Class	On Time?		Had materials?		Completed Work?		Self-Control			Teacher's Initials
	Yes	No	Yes	No	Yes	No	Excellent	Fair	Poor	
	☐ ☐	☐ ☐	☐ ☐	☐ ☐	☐ ☐	☐ ☐	☐ ☐	☐ ☐	☐ ☐	
	☐ ☐	☐ ☐	☐ ☐	☐ ☐	☐ ☐	☐ ☐	☐ ☐	☐ ☐	☐ ☐	
	☐ ☐	☐ ☐	☐ ☐	☐ ☐	☐ ☐	☐ ☐	☐ ☐	☐ ☐	☐ ☐	
	☐ ☐	☐ ☐	☐ ☐	☐ ☐	☐ ☐	☐ ☐	☐ ☐	☐ ☐	☐ ☐	
	☐ ☐	☐ ☐	☐ ☐	☐ ☐	☐ ☐	☐ ☐	☐ ☐	☐ ☐	☐ ☐	

Self-Control Key:

Excellent
1. Consistently followed classroom rules.
2. Spoke respectfully to others.
3. Did not threaten or aggress physically.
4. Interacted positively with peers and adults at all times.

Fair
1. Followed classroom rules most of the time.
2. Spoke respectfully to others some of the time.
3. Interacted positively with peers and adults some of the time.

Poor
1. Did not follow classroom rules.
2. Was not respectful to others.
3. Interacted negatively with peers or adults.

© 2012 by PRO-ED, Inc.   #13936

Weekly Monitoring

This form is appropriate for older students. Eight key behaviors that indicate self-regulation and self-control are listed for each day of the week.

Directions

The teacher should check Yes or No to indicate whether the student demonstrated each appropriate behavior within a class period. Comments can be written in the Daily Comments section. Review progress with the student at the end of each day. Discuss the student's behavior, provide feedback, and problem solve. At the end of the week, compute he total number of Yes and No checks and the percentage of each. Review with the student, and use the data to measure progress.

Weekly Monitoring Sheet

Student Name _____   Date _____

Teacher Name _____   Class or Time of Day _____

Behaviors	Yes	No	Daily Comments
Monday			
Followed directions from adults			
Brought books and materials			
Acted respectfully to peers and adults			
Completed assigned work			
Worked without disturbing others			
Remained in seat			
Respected personal boundaries, rights, and property of others			
Took responsibility for his/her own actions			
Tuesday			
Followed directions from adults			
Brought books and materials			
Acted respectfully to peers and adults			
Completed assigned work			
Worked without disturbing others			
Remained in seat			
Respected personal boundaries, rights, and property of others			
Took responsibility for his/her own actions			
Wednesday			
Followed directions from adults			
Brought books and materials			
Acted respectfully to peers and adults			
Completed assigned work			
Worked without disturbing others			
Remained in seat			
Respected personal boundaries, rights, and property of others			
Took responsibility for his/her own actions			
Thursday			
Followed directions from adults			
Brought books and materials			
Acted respectfully to peers and adults			
Completed assigned work			
Worked without disturbing others			
Remained in seat			
Respected personal boundaries, rights, and property of others			
Took responsibility for his/her own actions			
Friday			
Followed directions from adults			
Brought books and materials			
Acted respectfully to peers and adults			
Completed assigned work			
Worked without disturbing others			
Remained in seat			
Respected personal boundaries, rights, and property of others			
Took responsibility for his/her own actions			

© 2012 by PRO-ED, Inc.   #13936

Earn It/Lose It

The Earn/Lose It form provides a tool for monitoring student behavior and for applying consequences, that is, positive reinforcement for appropriate behavior and the removal of points for misbehavior. Each day, the student can earn or lose points by displaying either positive behaviors or problem behaviors. The point total is tallied at the end of the week, and the student can exchange points for items at a class store. Send this form home to the parent at the end of the week to be signed.

Directions

Provide points to the student for demonstrating specific behaviors. Put a tally mark by each behavior observed during a class period. For young students who stay in the same class all day, provide one point per subject. Positive points are added to a total available for spending in the class store. Subtract points for problem behaviors.

Earn It/Lose It

Student Name _____ Date _____ to _____

Earn points for these positive behaviors.

Positive Behaviors	Mon.	Tues.	Wed.	Thurs.	Fri.
1. Following adults' directions.					
2. Expressing feelings with words.					
3. Accepting correction or criticism.					
4. Cooperating with other students.					
5. Taking responsibility for own actions.					

Lose points for these problem behaviors.

Problem Behaviors	Mon.	Tues.	Wed.	Thurs.	Fri.
1. Threatening or hurting someone.					
2. Taking or destroying others' property.					
3. Leaving seat or work area.					
4. Interrupting instruction.					
5. Refusing to follow directions.					

Week's Total Positive Behavior Points [ ] − **Week's Total Problem Behavior Points** [ ] = **Final Total Points** [ ]

Parent Signature _____

© 2012 by PRO-ED, Inc.   #13936

Earn It/Lose It (Example)

Student Name _____ Date _____ to _____

Earn points for these positive behaviors.

Positive Behaviors	Mon.	Tues.	Wed.	Thurs.	Fri.
1. Following adults' directions.		/	///		
2. Expressing feelings with words.	//	/	/		/
3. Accepting correction or criticism.				/	
4. Cooperating with other students.	///				//
5. Taking responsibility for own actions.					

Lose points for these problem behaviors.

Problem Behaviors	Mon.	Tues.	Wed.	Thurs.	Fri.
1. Threatening or hurting someone.		/			
2. Taking or destroying others' property.					
3. Leaving seat or work area.	///			/	
4. Interrupting instruction.	/	/			/
5. Refusing to follow directions.					

Week's Total Positive Behavior Points [15] − Week's Total Problem Behavior Points [8] = Final Total Points [7]

Parent Signature _____

© 2012 by PRO-ED, Inc.   #13936

Self-Monitoring Tool

Before students can control and regulate their behavior, they must be aware of it and monitor themselves. Teach students to monitor their own behavior by encouraging them to use the Self-Monitoring Tool. Before they begin, explain why it is important and how improving self-management will be beneficial. Model self-talk, and explain how students can use the tool to evaluate themselves on specific behaviors. Two forms are provided, one for younger students and one for older students.

Directions

1. Describe a behavior you would like to see students enact in class. Use an action verb to describe the behavior. Here are some common expectations:
   - Help other students in your group.
   - Keep your hands to yourself.
2. Teach students to review their own behavior by modeling self-talk. Use phrases such as the following:
   - Am I helping my friends?
   - Am I touching only my own things?

Halfway through the activity, say the phrase for students, and then ask them to repeat it to be sure they are staying focused on their behavior.

3. Give students an opportunity to practice silently asking themselves the question.
4. When students have completed the lesson or activity, suggest that they ask themselves how they did on the specific behaviors. After they silently ask the question, they can fill out the self-monitoring form.
5. Use the forms as the basis for discussion and feedback with the entire class or individual students. Help students improve their self-monitoring, and teach them to set goals for improvement.

Note. This idea is adapted from *Practical Ideas That Really Work for Students with Disruptive, Defiant, or Difficult Behaviors: Preschool Through Grade 4* (2nd ed., pp. 145–146), by K. McConnell, G. R. Ryser, and J. R. Patton, 2010, Austin, TX: PRO-ED. Copyright 2010 by PRO-ED, Inc. Reprinted with permission.

Self-Monitoring

How did I do on _____?

(Circle a number)

3	2	1
Great	Okay	Not very well

What I did well

_____

What should I do even better next time?

_____

Self-Monitoring

How did I do on _____?

(Circle a picture)

☺ 😐 ☹
Great   Okay   Not very well

What I did well

_____

What should I do even better next time?

_____

© 2012 by PRO-ED, Inc.   #13936

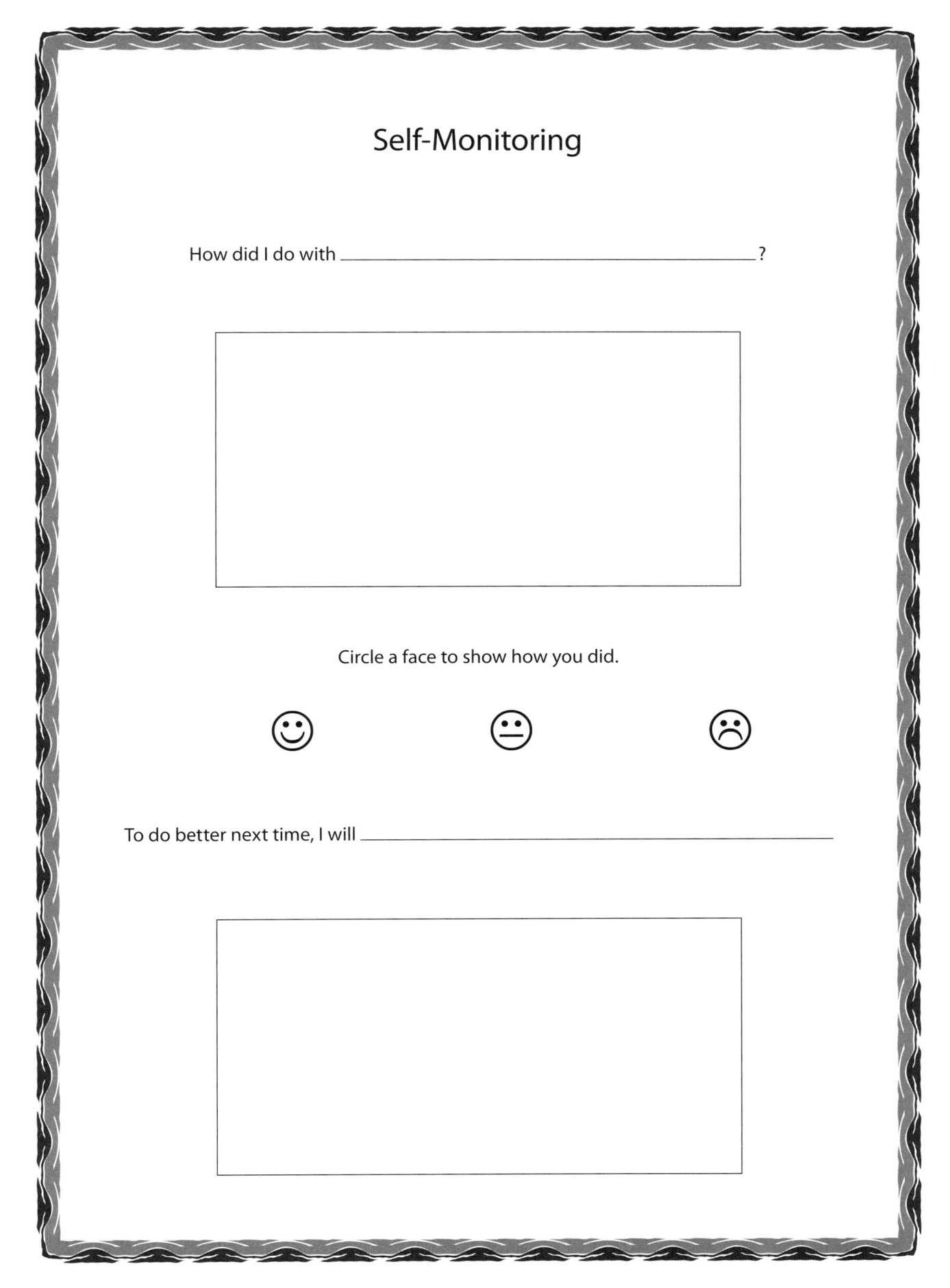

Self-Monitoring

How did I do with _____?

Circle a face to show how you did.

☺   ☻   ☹

To do better next time, I will _____

© 2012 by PRO-ED, Inc. #13936

Self-Regulation Progress

Self-regulation and key behaviors related to it are critical in group situations. The Self-Regulation Progress form can be used to closely monitor a student's performance on self-regulation skills.

Directions

At the top of this form, write the target behavior that will be monitored. Determine a percentage that will earn a reward and a percentage that will result in a consequence, and write those numbers in the blanks. Next, add a reward the student will earn if he or she shows the targeted behavior for the determined percentage of the day. Then, add a consequence if the student does not show the targeted behavior for the determined percentage of the day.

The chart divides the day into time slots rather than subject periods. Rate the student according to his or her demonstration of the target behavior after each time period has ended. The Comments column provides space to make statements about the student's effort. Calculate the percentage at the end of the marking period. The student can take the chart home to show off his or her accomplishment to parents.

Self-Regulation Progress

Student Name _____ Date _____

Target self-regulation behavior: _____

Reward for at least _____ % is _____

Consequence for less than _____ % is _____

Time	Self-Regulation Behavior	Comments
	❏ Yes ❏ No	
	❏ Yes ❏ No	
	❏ Yes ❏ No	
	❏ Yes ❏ No	
	❏ Yes ❏ No	
	❏ Yes ❏ No	
	❏ Yes ❏ No	
	❏ Yes ❏ No	
	❏ Yes ❏ No	
	❏ Yes ❏ No	
	❏ Yes ❏ No	
	❏ Yes ❏ No	
	❏ Yes ❏ No	
	❏ Yes ❏ No	

# of Yes ÷ Total Possible × 100 = % Yes

© 2012 by PRO-ED, Inc.   #13936

Self-Regulation Progress (Example)

Student Name __Janelle Harrison__ Date __5/1/12__

Target self-regulation behavior: __Ask for help when frustrated or upset__

Reward for at least __70__ % is __free time on the computer__

Consequence for less than __40__ % is __I will write my plan for reaching this goal.__

Time	Self-Regulation Behavior	Comments
8:00–8:30	☐ Yes ☑ No	J. became upset when asked to redo assignments.
8:30–9:00	☑ Yes ☐ No	
9:00–9:30	☑ Yes ☐ No	
9:30–10:00	☑ Yes ☐ No	
10:00–10:30	☑ Yes ☐ No	
10:30–11:00	☑ Yes ☐ No	
11:00–11:30	☑ Yes ☐ No	
11:30–12:00	☑ Yes ☐ No	
12:00–12:30	☑ Yes ☐ No	
12:30–1:00	☑ Yes ☐ No	
1:00–1:30	☐ Yes ☑ No	J. did not ask for help with math assignment.
1:30–2:00	☑ Yes ☐ No	
2:00–2:30	☑ Yes ☐ No	
2:30–3:00	☑ Yes ☐ No	

# of Yes ÷ Total Possible × 100 = % Yes

To Reach My Goal

Goals need to be SPECIFIC. For example, the goal "I want my classmates to respect me" is not specific. The goal "I will make eye contact when I walk in the classroom and see my classmates and smile at them" is specific. Asking more detailed questions is the best technique for establishing specific goals. A helpful question is, "What will you be doing differently when this is no longer a problem?"

SCALING is a useful tool to get the student to think about the present situation in specifics. It also communicates the message that we expect that there will be measurable progress. Scaling questions can be framed in a number of ways. The basic format is, "On a scale of one to five, with one being the worst this situation could be and five being the best the situation could be, what number describes where it is today?"

Goals should be OBSERVABLE. When we ask students to tell us what a behavior on a point on the scale looks like, they can describe the behavior in operational, concrete terms that we can all agree on.

Directions

On the monitoring sheet "To Reach My Goal," ask the student to list a goal as specifically as possible—one that you can observe. You can help the student by asking questions such as, "What will I see you doing when you are _____?" Then have the student scale where he or she is currently regarding the goal behavior. Finally, have the student describe what a "5" would look and sound like as a way to operationalize the goal and keep it very concrete.

To Reach My Goal

Name _____ Date _____

My goal is: _____

_____

At this time, I am doing:

1	2	3	4	5
Terrible	Pretty Bad	Okay	Pretty Good	Great

To be a "5" and do great, what I will do and say:

Looks Like This	Sounds Like This

© 2012 by PRO-ED, Inc.   #13936

To Reach My Goal (Example)

Name: Drew Ellis   Date: October 20th

My goal is: talk to other students in ways that are comfortable for them, including standing at a good distance, using a voice that is loud enough for the setting, and keeping my hands to myself.

At this time, I am doing:

1	2	3	4	5
Terrible	Pretty Bad	Okay	Pretty Good	Great
	X			

To be a "5" and do great, what I will do and say:

Looks Like This	Sounds Like This
I ask an adult to observe the other student's body language to let me know if he is comfortable with how close I am, how loud my voice is, and my body language.	Could you help me work on some people skills by noticing the reactions of the person I'm talking to?
I watch how far away students are standing from each other and stand about the same distance.	

53   © 2012 by PRO-ED, Inc.   #13936

Behavior Improvement Drawings

When students self-monitor their classroom behaviors, it promotes self-responsibility and frees the teacher from having to interrupt instruction to note behavior ratings. The behaviors selected for this monitoring tool should be very specific and simple so the student can clearly judge whether the appropriate behavior has occurred. Keys to success include a short time span (a timer is useful), a clear understanding by the student of what the behavior looks like, and a method for marking the occurrence that is not disruptive to the instructional setting.

Directions

Establish a clear, simple behavioral goal with the student, such as "keeping my hands to myself." Use this behavior as the title at the top of the student's worksheet. Plan to set a timer or some other method for the student to see and note the time intervals. For example, a student who is working on keeping his hands to himself might set a small timer for 15 minutes. When the alert goes off, he determines if he has kept his hands to himself during that time interval and, if so, marks the next section of the drawing and resets the timer. When the drawing is complete, the student can color the picture and take it home.

Name _____ Date _____
Behavior Title _____

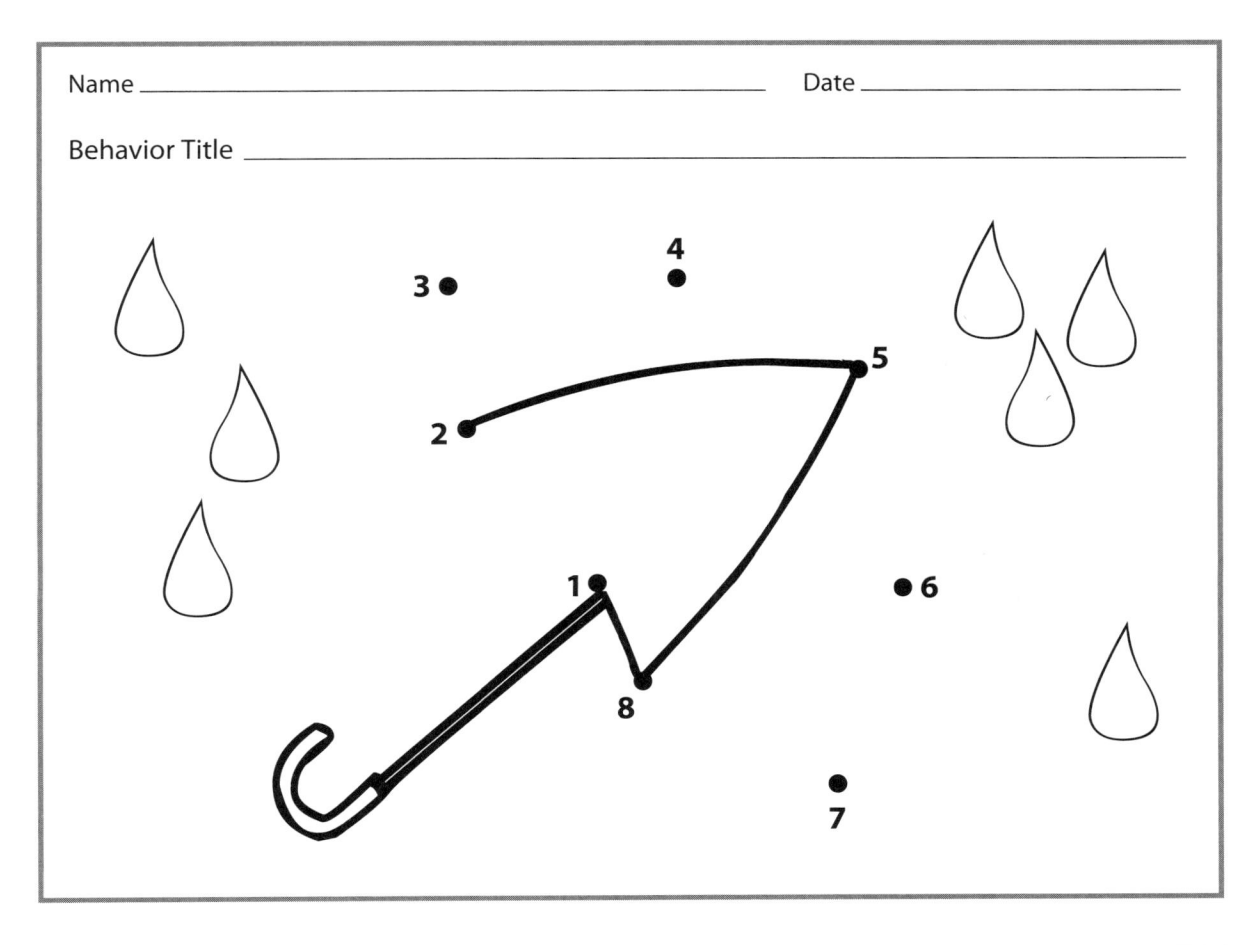

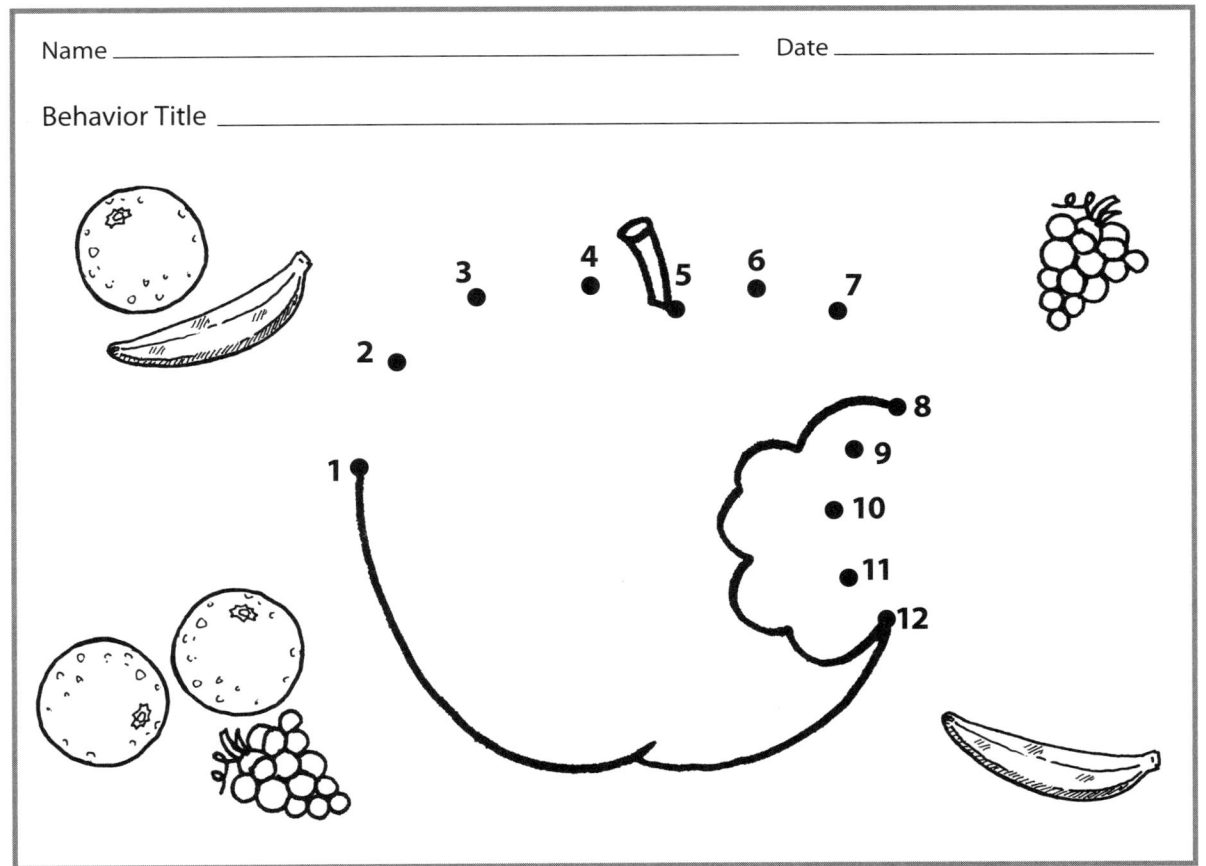

Name _____ Date _____
Behavior Title _____

© 2012 by PRO-ED, Inc.   #13936

Name _____ Date _____

Behavior Title _____

Name _____ Date _____

Behavior Title _____

© 2012 by PRO-ED, Inc.   #13936

Check Off My Progress!

When students take charge of marking their attempts to practice a new behavior, they become more responsible for their behavior.

Directions

With the student, identify a behavior to practice often that will move the student toward positive behavior change. Make sure the behavior you agree on is observable, small, and specific. Set a realistic time span for the student to report on the behavior, beginning with shorter intervals and moving toward longer intervals as the student increases the goal behavior. Designate a reward, if desired, for the student upon completion of a specified number of behavior occurrences.

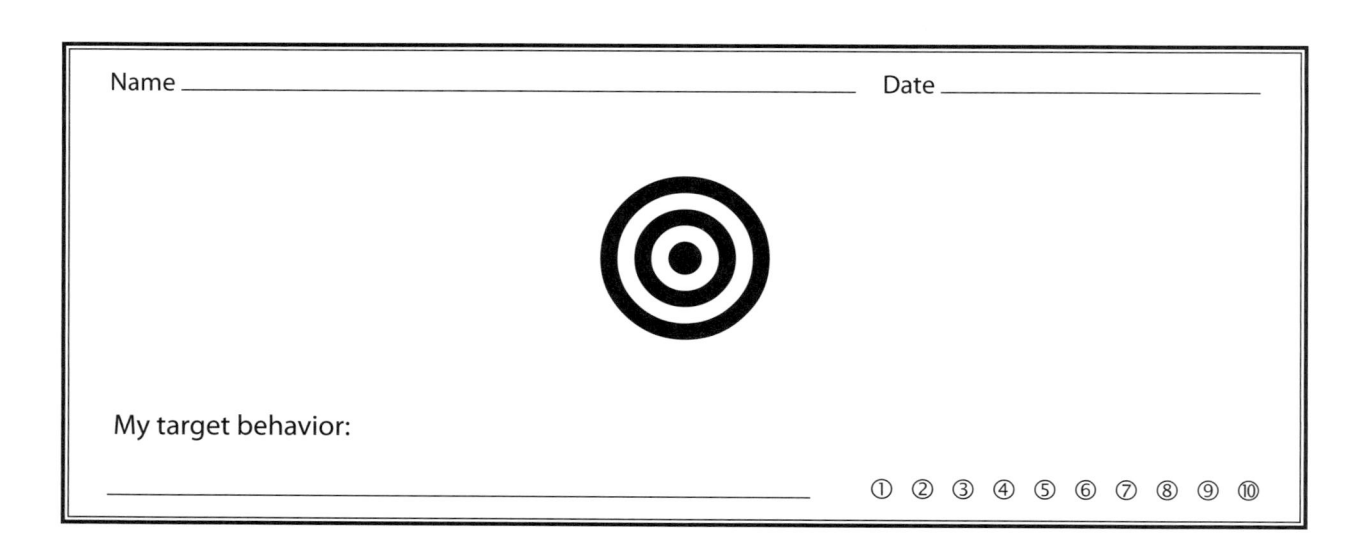

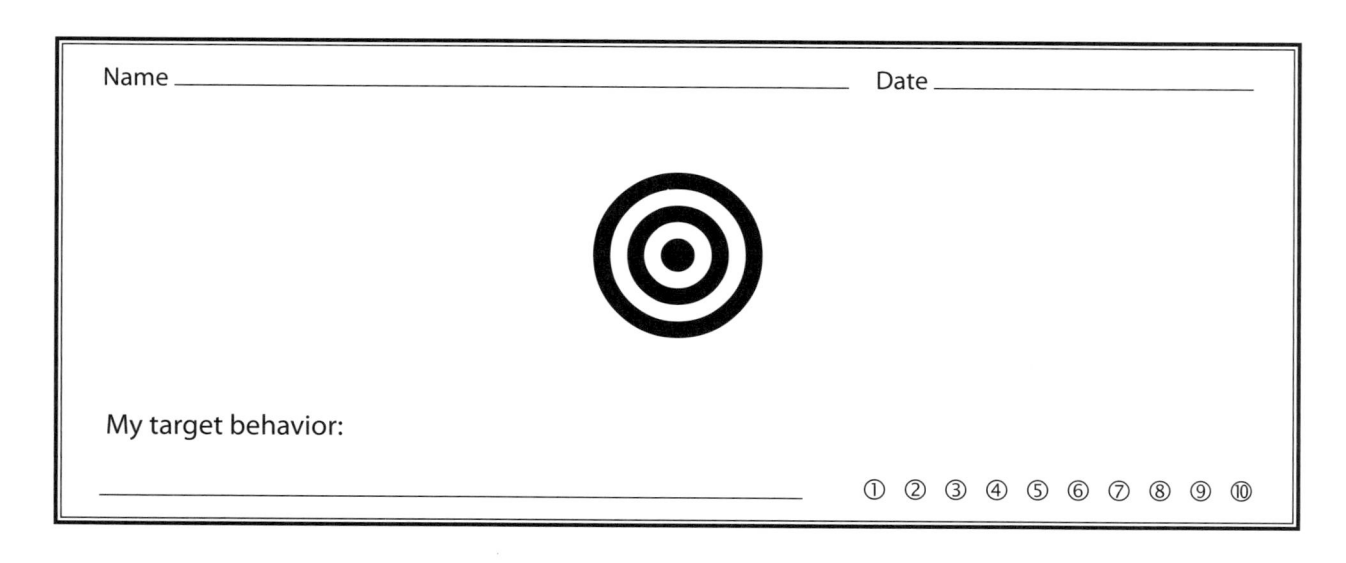

Name _____ Date _____

My target behavior:

_____ ① ② ③ ④ ⑤ ⑥ ⑦ ⑧ ⑨ ⑩

Name _____ Date _____

My target behavior:

_____ ① ② ③ ④ ⑤ ⑥ ⑦ ⑧ ⑨ ⑩

Name _____ Date _____

My target behavior:

_____ ① ② ③ ④ ⑤ ⑥ ⑦ ⑧ ⑨ ⑩

© 2012 by PRO-ED, Inc. #13936

Goal Setting

Having students define their own goals for behavior improvement is part of the solution-focused approach. When students articulate their goal, they shift the locus of control from external to internal. It can be a step toward students taking self-responsibility.

Students do not always agree with adults' ideas for behavior goals and may resist complying. Frequently, though, students can identify things they could do differently that would make a positive difference for them at school. They may surprise you! This line of questioning allows students to describe changes in terms of something they can do. Typically, students suggest solutions they can actually deliver.

Directions

Use the Goal Setting monitoring form to help students describe their best hope for behavior change. When we ask them to describe when that is happening, if even for a little bit, we shift their focus from the problem to the solution. Understanding what is happening when things are a little bit better gives clues to how to get it to happen more often. Asking students to describe the first small sign of progress puts things in observable terms. Asking students what differences their behavior progress will make for them helps them visualize the benefit and gives them reasons to continue to work for progress.

Name _____   Date _____

Goal Setting

What could you be doing differently that would make a difference in school for you?

_____

_____

_____

What's your best hope for things improving at school?

_____

_____

_____

When is that happening, if even for a little bit?

_____

_____

_____

When you are working on your goal, what will be the first small sign that you are making progress toward your goal?

_____

_____

_____

What difference will it make for you when that happens?

_____

_____

_____

_____

© 2012 by PRO-ED, Inc.   #13936

Name: Eva   Date: October 15

Goal Setting (Example)

What could you be doing differently that would make a difference in school for you?

Instead of getting mad at the teacher or my group when I don't understand, I could ask for help when I first begin to get confused.

What's your best hope for things improving at school?

I could always stay calm and get help when I need it and not be thought of as the "kid who always blows."

When is that happening, if even for a little bit?

In science lab, I am usually able to show my group where I first start to be a little confused by checking the steps of the lab as I go.

When you are working on your goal, what will be the first small sign that you are making progress toward your goal?

I will tell others in a calm voice that I need some additional explanation, and on my own I will go back to the point before I became confused.

What difference will it make for you when that happens?

I will stay calm and be better able to understand when I do get another explanation. I'll get my work done and not be teased by other students.

Contract Ideas

Use the form Contract Ideas to elicit input from teachers and others who know the student to create effective behavior goals. When teachers can describe the desired behavior in action terms, everyone has a clearer idea of what needs to happen.

More often than not, the student is already exhibiting the desired behavior, at least sometimes, in certain settings, or under certain circumstances. Identifying those times and examining what is going on can help find factors to increase the behavior. Usually, even the most seriously acting-out student has some behaviors that are worth reinforcing. Ask the referring person to help identify those and to think about what the student will be doing when behavior improves.

To be effective, a goal should be a SMALL STEP. "Mary will stop having arguments with her friend Shelley" requires too many steps to be one goal. "Mary will wear the bracelet her grandmother gave her each day for a week to remind her to smile when she sees Shelley" could be a goal for Mary. Questions like, "What will be the first signs that _____ (problem) has improved?" lead to goals that are small steps.

Finally, ask the referring person to think about what difference the student's behavior improvement will make. Goals must be MEANINGFUL AND RELEVANT to the student to be effective. "Eddie will do his assigned social studies reading next week" may be a very meaningful goal to the adults in Eddie's environment and not to him, yet, "Eddie will ask his mother to sit with him for thirty minutes while he reads his social studies assignment" will have meaning for him if his goal is to have more time with his mother.

Student's Name _____ Date _____

Person Completing Form _____

Contract Ideas

Behavior goal: _____

_____

What helps the student to have the desired behavior?

_____

_____

What is the student already doing that you would like to see continue?

_____

_____

When the behavior of concern improves, what will the student be doing instead?

_____

_____

What will be the first small signs that the student's behavior is improving?

1. _____

2. _____

3. _____

What difference will it make when the student's behavior improves, even for a little bit?

_____

_____

_____

© 2012 by PRO-ED, Inc.   #13936

Student's Name George Walker   Date September 29

Person Completing Form Ms. Simpson

Contract Ideas (Example)

Behavior goal: George will ask for help appropriately and remain calm while waiting for assistance to arrive.

What helps the student to have the desired behavior?
When I make it clear that the assignment is difficult and that help is available to the student by raising his hand.

What is the student already doing that you would like to see continue?
In Math, George has been able to circle the point in the material where he last understood.

When the behavior of concern improves, what will the student be doing instead?
George will be able to stay calm even when classwork is difficult and will be able to wait his turn for help.

What will be the first small signs that the student's behavior is improving?
1. George will suggest an appropriate signal to use with the teacher when he begins to need help.
2. George will use his personal calming technique to keep his cool.
3. George will backtrack to find the place in the work where he understood the material.

What difference will it make when the student's behavior improves, even for a little bit?
When George is able to stay calm and wait for help with his assignments, it will affect his relationships with his teachers and his classmates. He will experience better, calmer, and more productive days.

© 2012 by PRO-ED, Inc.   #13936

Progress Toward Goal

It is helpful for students to see a visual of progress made toward the completion of a behavioral goal. This goal chart allows students to mark their progress for each time increment. For example, the student could evaluate on a daily basis where his or her behavior is on a scale from 1 to 10, with 10 being the most desirable.

Example

Rating										
10										▓
9									▓	▓
8									▓	▓
7								▓	▓	▓
6						▓	▓	▓	▓	▓
5				▓		▓	▓	▓	▓	▓
4				▓	▓	▓	▓	▓	▓	▓
3			▓	▓	▓	▓	▓	▓	▓	▓
2		▓	▓	▓	▓	▓	▓	▓	▓	▓
1	▓	▓	▓	▓	▓	▓	▓	▓	▓	▓
	1	2	3	4	5	6	7	8	9	10

Days

Name _____   Date _____

Progress Toward Goal

My Goal (observable, concrete, positive, small): _____

_____

Progress toward my goal on a scale of 1 to 10 for each time period below:

10										
9										
8										
7										
6										
5										
4										
3										
2										
1										
	1	2	3	4	5	6	7	8	9	10

Rating (y-axis)

_____
(Sessions, Days, or other Time Increments)

© 2012 by PRO-ED, Inc.

Notice the Pattern

Students who show verbal or physical aggression often follow a pattern of behaviors that leads to outbursts or explosions. It is a good idea to intervene early with these students. First identify the steps in the aggressive behavior pattern. When you observe the telltale signs that student aggression is about to occur, you can intervene and prevent or minimize the aggression.

This tool includes suggestions for tracking the student's aggressive behavior pattern and strategies for interrupting that pattern before the aggression occurs. When used consistently, strategies like these often prevent agitation from becoming aggression.

Directions

1. Use the Find the Pattern form to help identify the pattern of behaviors that leads to aggression. Observe the student each time he or she demonstrates aggression, or better yet, have another adult observe the student. Complete the form immediately after the aggressive incident occurs.

2. Combine the information from several observations, and try to identify the pattern that leads to the student's aggressive behavior.

3. Summarize the frequency and severity of the student's aggression.

4. Intervene before the outburst or explosion occurs by completing the provided Intervene on the Pattern form, and then implement your plan to redirect or calm the student before he or she shows aggression.

5. Use your plan for 3 to 6 weeks, and review the number and severity of the student's aggressive incidents.

6. Revise your plan and try again if needed.

Note. This idea is adapted from *Practical Ideas That Really Work for Students with Disruptive, Defiant, or Difficult Behaviors: Preschool Through Grade 4* (2nd ed., pp. 129–131), by K. McConnell, G. R. Ryser, and J. R. Patton, 2010, Austin, TX: PRO-ED. Copyright 2010 by PRO-ED, Inc. Reprinted with permission.

Find the Pattern

Student _____ Date _____

Day of the Week _____ Time of Day _____

The student's aggression included:

- ❏ Verbal threats
- ❏ Cursing
- ❏ Hitting or grabbing
- ❏ Spitting
- ❏ Kicking
- ❏ Throwing things
- ❏ Destroying property
- ❏ Turning over furniture
- ❏ Other: _____

The student's aggression was directed at:

- ❏ Adults, especially
- ❏ Students, especially
- ❏ Both

Before the aggression, here is what was happening:

- ❏ The student got a direction to _____.
- ❏ The student transitioned from _____ to _____.
- ❏ The student was working on _____.
- ❏ The student was working with _____.
- ❏ The environmental conditions included _____.
- ❏ The student had difficulty with _____.
- ❏ The student was told "no" when _____.
- ❏ The student _____.

Before the aggression, here is how the student looked, sounded, or acted:

- ❏ The student had a flushed face or neck.
- ❏ The student clenched his or her fists.
- ❏ The student was talking in a louder or softer voice than normal.
- ❏ The student was crying, laughing, or whining.
- ❏ The student averted gaze or used a direct, challenging gaze.
- ❏ The student demonstrated unusual or excessive movement.
  Describe: _____
- ❏ The student's speech was disjointed, rapid, or confused.
- ❏ The student refused a request or direction.
- ❏ The student _____.

The total number of aggressive incidents from _____ to _____ has been _____.

© 2012 by PRO-ED, Inc.   #13936

Intervene on the Pattern

Before the aggression, the student's pattern includes:

_____

_____

_____

_____

_____

My plan is to intervene by:

- ❏ Redirecting the student to get a drink of water or go to the bathroom.
- ❏ Using visual cues or nonverbal signals directing the student to calm down.
- ❏ Talking to the student alone in the hall.
- ❏ Signaling the student to move to a quiet area of the classroom.
- ❏ Asking the student to run an errand or complete a chore.
- ❏ Giving the student a routine assignment (e.g., copy something, sort something, or organize something).
- ❏ Using a time-out or calm-down routine the student has developed.
- ❏ Giving the student a choice between two activities or tasks.
- ❏ Cuing the student to take deep breaths.
- ❏ Using a timer or hourglass, and asking the student to watch it for 2 to 5 minutes.
- ❏ Calling another adult to come to the classroom.
- ❏ Reminding the student that I care, and repeating what I want the student to do.
- ❏ Removing the other students from the classroom.

Other: _____

_____

_____

_____

_____

Chapter 4
Skill Units

Skill Unit 1: Describes physical sensations separately from emotions

Skill Unit 2: Expresses emotions verbally

Skill Unit 3: Accepts criticism and praise

Skill Unit 4: Takes responsibility for actions

Skill Unit 5: Initiates a calming strategy after being upset

Skill Unit 6: Follows directions from adults

Skill Unit 7: Responds to nonverbal cues

Skill Unit 8: Demonstrates empathy for others

Skill Unit 9: Works productively in a group

Skill Unit 10: Identifies consequences before acting

Skill Unit 11: Manages transitions

Skill Unit 12: Uses resources for obtaining help when getting upset

Skill Unit 13: Attends to task, ignores distractions

Skill Unit 14: Respects personal boundaries, rights, and property of others

Skill Unit 15: Negotiates with others when there is disagreement

Skill Unit 1
Describes physical sensations separately from emotions

Background Information

Kids often pay little or no attention to the physical sensations in their bodies. They may experience a sensation, automatically jump to attributing an emotion to that sensation, and then follow a pattern of behavior associated with that emotion that gets them into trouble. Kids who learn to identify physical sensations can isolate and address these sensations before the emotion–behavior pattern happens. Levine (1997); Saxe, Ellis, and Kaplow (2007); and Ogden, Minton, and Pain (2006) suggested that the capacity to track sensations is an internal resource that students can use to alert themselves to the need to ground. Kids can learn easy and effective strategies for coping with sensations that can be used in all environments.

Activities and Strategies

Before helping kids become aware of their physical sensations, spend time teaching them some simple calming routines, such as breathing and grounding. These routines can protect kids from becoming too aroused when they reflect on emotions that are associated with the physical sensations.

Next, teach kids to be mindfully aware—that is, be fully aware in the moment, not judging or evaluating, just noticing what is there.

- Develop mindful awareness of the external environment with games, such as I Spy.
- Develop mindful awareness of a simple experience, such as eating chocolate or a raisin.

Teach kids to notice the physical sensations in their body as being separate from the ways they have learned to describe emotions.

- Notice the current sensations in your own body. Describe and list terms on the board.
- Have the students describe or illustrate the times they have felt various sensations, such as
  - tingling,
  - being hot, or
  - having butterflies.
- Give kids simple emotional scenarios they can identify with (e.g., scary, angry, happy, anxious), and ask them to focus on and describe their sensations.
- Once kids can identify sensations, teach them to track the movement of the sensation in their bodies by focusing on it and noticing when it moves through their bodies. Tracking sensations allows for a mindful awareness and nonjudgmental attitude toward a sensation.

SKILL UNIT 1: Body Cues

Targeted Skill:

Describes physical sensations separately from emotions.

Materials:

Signals of Stress handout; Strategy Cards handout

Why

The body is first to respond to stressful stimuli. When people encounter something that makes them upset, physiological processes such as blood pressure and heart rate increase and these bodily changes usually cause people to behave or act differently. Problems occur when people don't notice these changes until they become enraged and out of control.

When one is presented with an anger-provoking situation, the key to noticing changes in behavior and actions is to recognize the body cues for anger. When people recognize an identified body cue at the first sign of anger, it can help them control their anger more easily.

Before people can release physical sensations, such as stress, they have to recognize the signs in their bodies that announce that they are becoming upset. The "Body Cues" activity will help students name the physical sensations they feel when they are stressed or upset. Once students have the capacity for early identification of physical sensations, they can intervene before they attach emotions and the resultant problematic behaviors to those sensations.

How

The "Body Cues" activity works best with a student and adult who are in a calm, secure relationship. As the adult, check your own arousal state and reregulate to calmness before working with the student. Continue to be aware of the student's emotional state and of its effect on you, reregulating as necessary throughout your work with the student. Research shows that students are affected by adults' calm, so remember that "our calm begets calm."

1. Ask the student to sit down and say that you are going to do a short exercise to experience using somatic awareness. Say: **Please get comfortable in your chair. Notice, is your back resting against the back of the chair? Feel your feet planted firmly on the ground. Pay special attention to the sensation of your heels touching the floor. How are your shoulders feeling? Do you notice any internal physical feelings, like tension, pain, relaxation, or warmth? What's your skin temperature (cool, warm, hot, cold)? By checking in with your body, you have become more aware of your somatic experience in the moment.**

2. Next, ask the student to think about a recent time when he or she felt happy and safe. While the student is thinking

about that experience, ask the student to reflect on the following: **What was happening? Who was there? What made you happy? What made you feel safe? Remember as much as you can from that time, with as much detail as you can.** After a few moments, ask the student: **What did you notice in your body when you were feeling happy and safe? Do you notice any changes now? Are you more relaxed? Is there less tension in your muscles? Enjoy this moment and just notice how it feels in your body.**

3. Next, ask the student to think about a time within the past few days that he or she felt upset, frustrated, or nervous. Say: **You were really upset. You might have been worried, angry, or frightened. It might have been a person who upset you, a place—maybe at school, or a situation—like taking a test. Where were you? Who were you with? What was happening?**

4. **Now, thinking about that stressful time, think about how your body felt. How was your breathing, your heart rate? Were you hot or cold, tense or relaxed? Pay attention to the physical sensations in your body.**

5. **Now, take a long, slow breath and slowly allow yourself to return to the memory of being happy and safe. Notice what you feel in your body. As you are ready, come back into the present moment.**

6. Direct the student to the Signals of Stress handout. Say: **Sometimes we are able to notice how our bodies are reacting to stress. Let's look at the handout and check any of the feelings that happen in your body when you are beginning to get upset. Add any others that describe your feelings.**

7. Optional: Have the student think about where he or she feels the physical sensations. Use the three boxes in the handout.

Name _____ Date _____

Signals of Stress

- ❏ Jumpy
- ❏ Fidgety
- ❏ Fast breathing
- ❏ Shaky hands
- ❏ Cold hands
- ❏ Shaky legs
- ❏ Pounding and fast hearbeat
- ❏ Tightness in chest
- ❏ Dry mouth
- ❏ Teary eyes
- ❏ Upset stomach
- ❏ Sweating
- ❏ Headache
- ❏ Other _____

Signals of Happy and Safe

List some physical sensations you have in your body when you are feeling happy and safe:

_____
_____
_____
_____
_____
_____
_____

© 2012 by PRO-ED, Inc.   #13936

Name _____   Date _____

Strategy Cards

For each sensation, I notice:

Draw it.	Describe it. _____ _____ _____	What I can do about it: ▪ ▪ ▪
Draw it.	Describe it. _____ _____ _____	What I can do about it: ▪ ▪ ▪
Draw it.	Describe it. _____ _____ _____	What I can do about it: ▪ ▪ ▪
Draw it.	Describe it. _____ _____ _____	What I can do about it: ▪ ▪ ▪
Draw it.	Describe it. _____ _____ _____	What I can do about it: ▪ ▪ ▪

© 2012 by PRO-ED, Inc.   #13936

SKILL UNIT 1: Put Your Feelings on the Map

Targeted Skill:

Describes physical sensations separately from emotions.

Materials:

Body Maps

Why

Some people do not notice physical responses until the responses are intense and difficult to control. Teaching students, especially young students, to recognize how their bodies feel can be a useful step in preventing outbursts and meltdowns. They will still need to learn strategies for dealing with their internal feelings, but recognizing and describing the physical manifestations of those feelings are good ways to begin.

How

A Body Map is a simple, visual tool that will help students identify how they react physically to emotions caused by stressful situations and experiences. While working with students on this skill, make multiple copies of the Body Map, using either the blank version or the labeled version. You may also project this image on a screen when working with a group. This skill is best used in small groups because students can brainstorm some of their physical sensations and discuss them with others. Here is how to help students "put their feelings on the map."

1. Work with the student or students to identify an emotion they can understand. For younger students, use simple language and begin with simple emotions, such as happy, sad, or mad. After identifying the emotion, write it on the top line of the Body Map, after "Sometimes I feel . . . ."

2. Ask the student or students to identify situations, people, or external stressors that make them feel this way. Students can provide examples from school, home, or both.

3. After identifying their emotions and the causes of those emotions, work with students to identify how different parts of their bodies feel when they are experiencing the emotion. They can label their Body Map to explain those feelings. Encourage students to consider all different parts of their bodies and to recognize that different people have different physical reactions to the same emotion. Contrast the different physical reactions that some students feel. For younger students, keep your descriptors short and clear.

4. Discuss with students why it is important to recognize these physical feelings. Explain that sometimes they may experience the physical reactions before they recognize the emotions that cause them, and that by recognizing these physical reactions students can determine the emotion they are feeling

and begin to control it. If they can control their bodies, their emotions often can be expressed in nonaggressive ways.

Just in Case

Identifying the physical reactions that accompany emotions is not enough to prevent a student from reacting physically; however, physical reactions are useful cues that something intense or unpleasant is happening. When students learn to identify and control their physical sensations, they may prevent themselves from hurting someone or destroying property. Everyone experiences negative emotions from time to time, but managing the negative reactions caused by those emotions is essential. Teach students positive alternatives to expressing emotions in harmful ways.

Name _____   Date _____

Body Map

Sometimes I feel _____. Things that can make me feel this way are _____, _____, or _____.

When I am like this, my body feels like this:

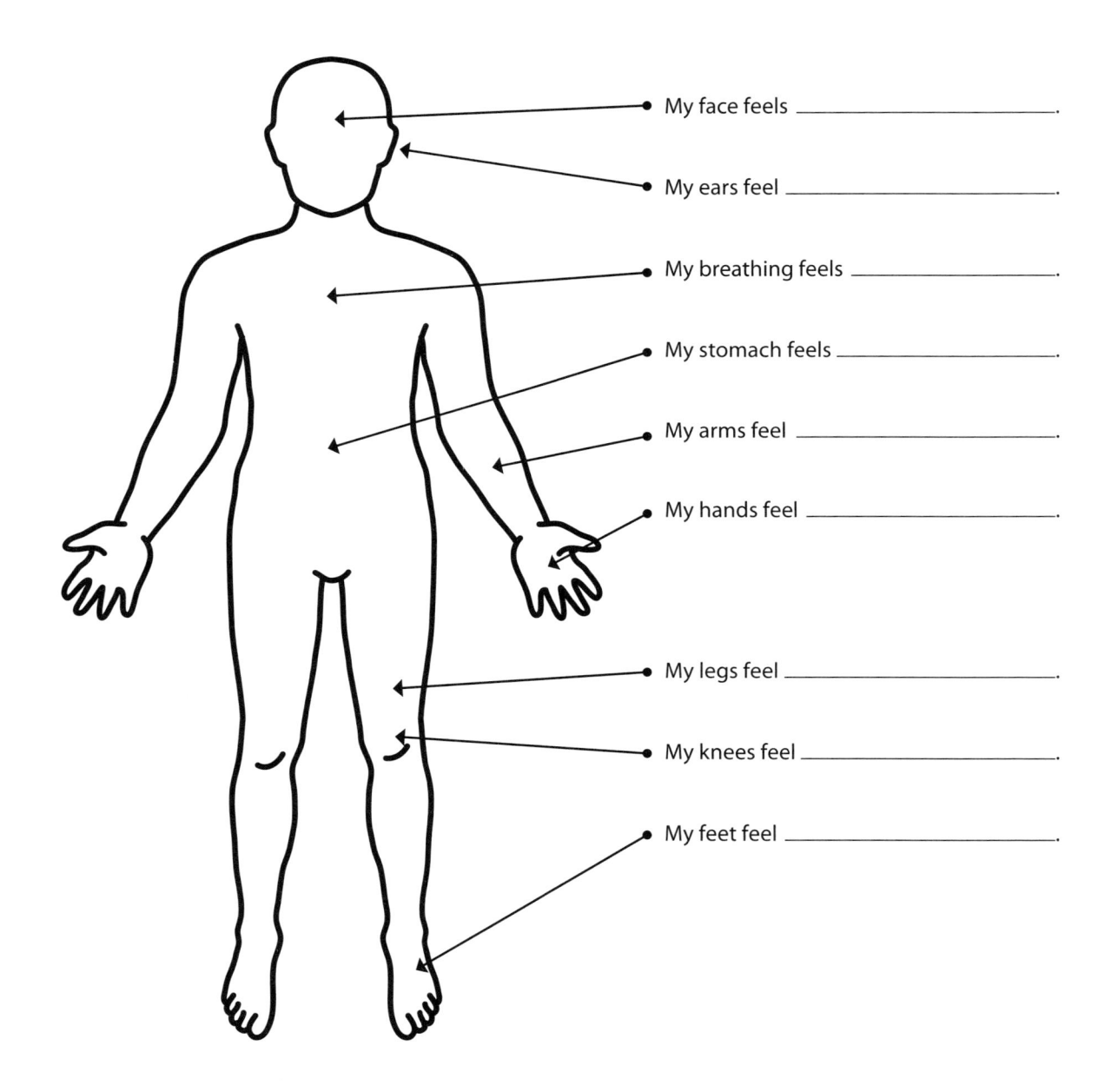

- My face feels _____.
- My ears feel _____.
- My breathing feels _____.
- My stomach feels _____.
- My arms feel _____.
- My hands feel _____.
- My legs feel _____.
- My knees feel _____.
- My feet feel _____.

© 2012 by PRO-ED, Inc.   #13936

Name _____   Date _____

Body Map

Sometimes I feel _____. Things that can make me feel this way are _____, _____, or _____.

When I am like this, my body feels like this:

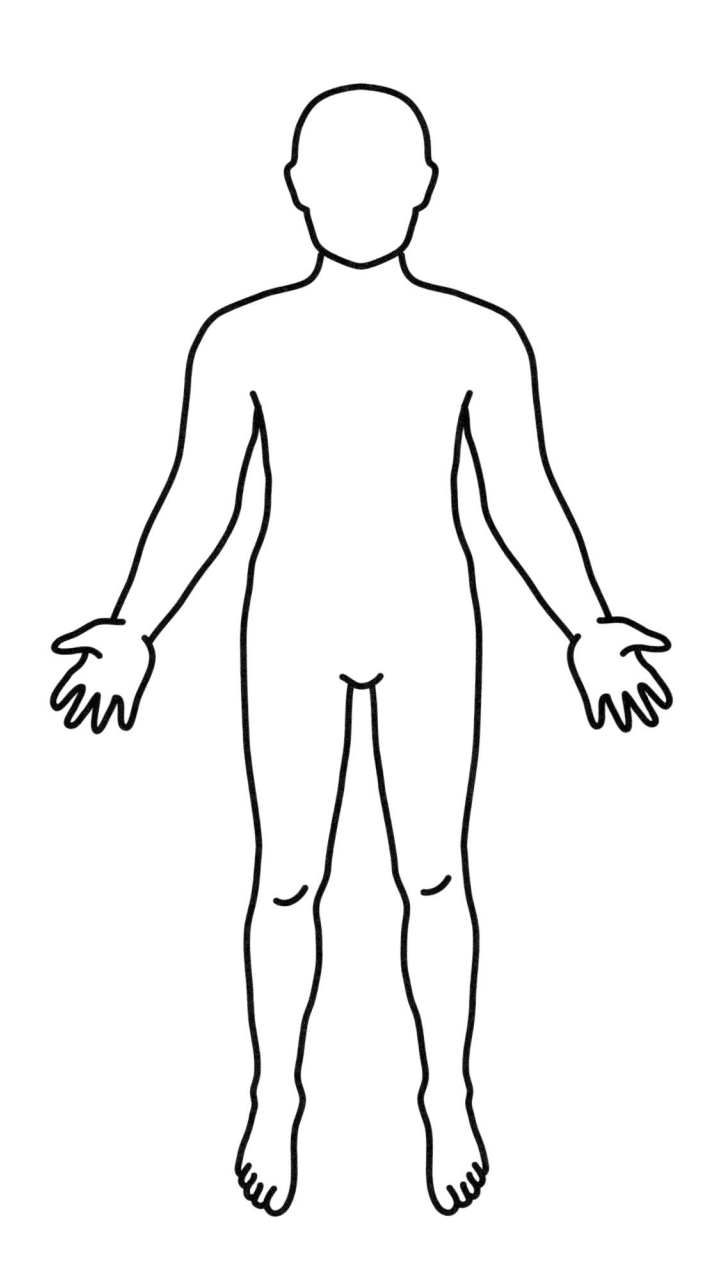

© 2012 by PRO-ED, Inc.   #13936

Name _____   Date _____

Body Map (Example)

Sometimes I feel _____angry_____. Things that can make me feel this way are _____teasing_____, _____pushing_____, or _____bad grade_____.

When I am like this, my body feels like this:

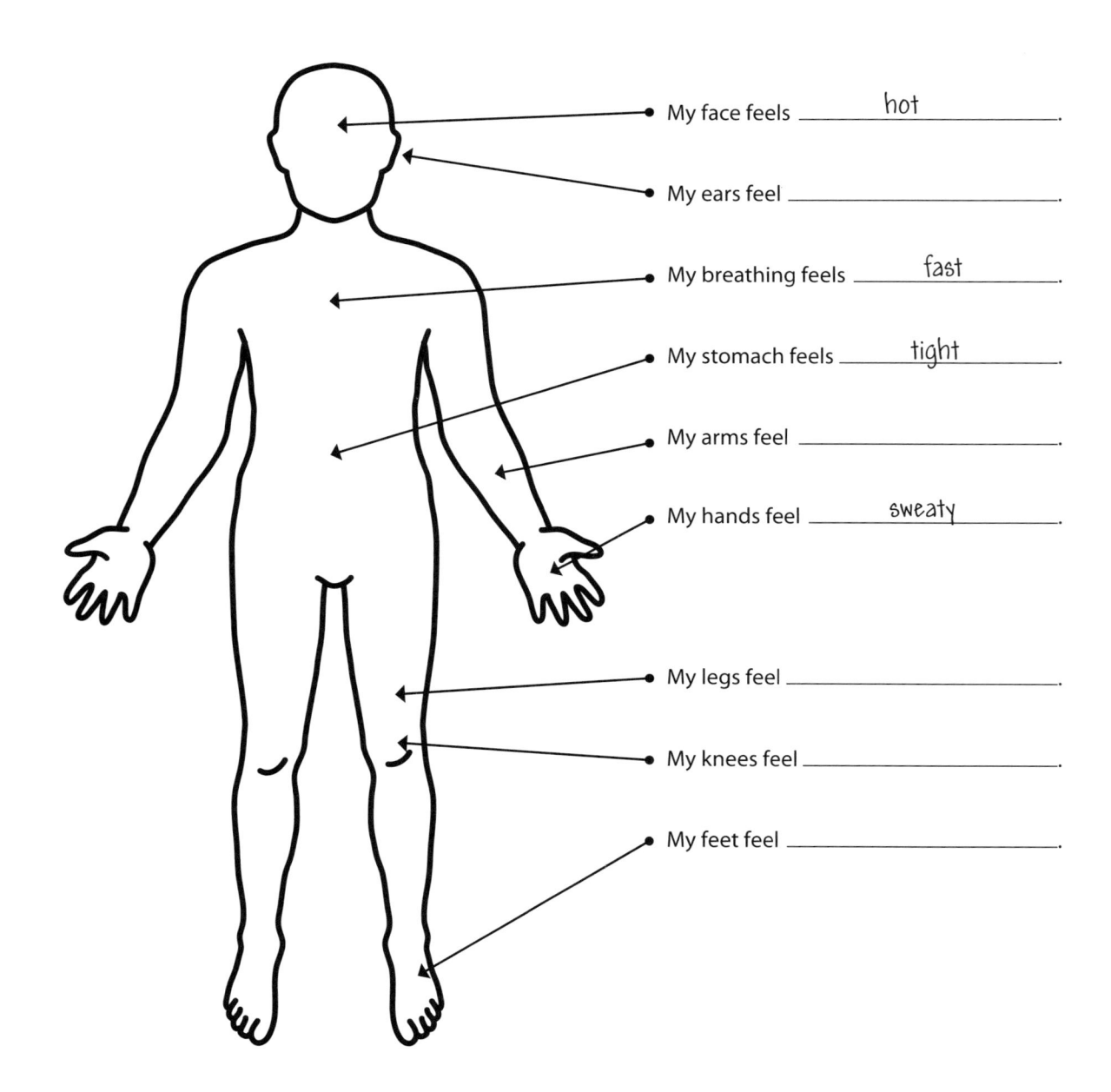

- My face feels _____hot_____.
- My ears feel _____.
- My breathing feels _____fast_____.
- My stomach feels _____tight_____.
- My arms feel _____.
- My hands feel _____sweaty_____.
- My legs feel _____.
- My knees feel _____.
- My feet feel _____.

© 2012 by PRO-ED, Inc.   #13936

SKILL UNIT 1: Table It

Targeted Skill:

Describes physical sensations separately from emotions.

Materials:

Table It forms

Why

Identifying one's own thoughts, emotions, and physical reactions are three separate, but closely linked, steps that are necessary for a positive and productive reaction to anxiety, anger, harm, or stress. Using a graphic organizer such as a table can help students who never considered these steps make sense of what is happening and generate positive responses. Use "Table It" when teaching students about the many dimensions of stressful situations, and use it as the basis for additional discussion and positive social skills practice. Help students focus on situations that are most difficult for them to deal with or that have led to problematic behavior in the past.

How

"Table It" can be used with a whole class, a small group, or individual students. If you are using the table with a large group, such as a whole class of students, remind them that everyone is different and not everyone reacts to specific situations in the same way. It is important, however, for individuals to know themselves so that they can continue to improve and make good choices in their reactions. Here is how to use the "Table It" activity.

1. Project a blank table, and give students individual copies.
2. Complete appropriate information for each section of the table. Model and explain for students as you complete each section. Differentiate each section so students understand the differences among them.
3. Let students explain things in their own words, but help them restate explanations if other students do not understand them.
4. When students make suggestions for completing the last column, explain to them that they do not need to have a complete answer or a perfect solution; just one productive, positive idea will help them get started to change things.

A partially completed table and a blank one are provided.

Just in Case

- You might need to help younger students understand the connections between what happens, what we think, what we feel, how we feel, and what we can do about it. It may be necessary to repeat the "Table It" activity several times, beginning with just one or two sections of the table and then talking about more situations or more complicated and difficult feelings. Help students think of at least one positive action, regardless of how small it might seem.

- When a student has managed him- or herself in an explosive situation, talk about the steps, what worked, and what to do more of next time.
- If a student has a serious behavior problem and has been aggressive, defiant, or extremely agitated, use the shortened version of the table as a problem-solving tool *after* an incident. An example is provided.

Name _____   Date _____

Table It (Example)

When I think...	I feel...	And my body...	To manage this, I can...
Someone is making fun of me.	Angry	Gets hot. My hands shake, and I make a mean face.	Tell an adult. Move away from the student.
I'm scared my parents might get divorced.			
	Worried		
		I have trouble breathing.	
	Tired		
	Anxious Scared		
I did something wrong and I might get caught.	Guilty Afraid		
		I get headaches.	
I am so sad I will never feel better.			
I eat too much and I can't stop.			
	Forgetful		
		Gets diarrhea or an upset stomach.	
		Can't sleep at night.	
I can't do anything right—ever.			
Nobody likes me.			

Name _____ Date _____

Table It

When I think . . .	I feel . . .	And my body . . .	To manage this, I can . . .

© 2012 by PRO-ED, Inc.   #13936

Name _____ Date _____

Table It Problem Solver/Success Recorder

When I think . . .	I feel . . .	And my body . . .	To manage this, I can . . .

© 2012 by PRO-ED, Inc.   #13936

Skill Unit 2
Expresses emotions verbally

Background Information

Students' abilities to understand how emotions affect them and to manage challenging situations affect learning and test performance (Zins, Weissberg, Wang, & Walberg, 2004). Kids often have no emotion vocabulary or have vocabulary that is limited to words such as *sad*, *mad*, and *glad*. Teaching kids to identify emotion and expand their descriptive vocabulary can help them let others know how they feel and what they need. Students who are able to name their emotions can acknowledge feeling those emotions and choose their behavior. Identifying emotions early on can allow kids (and others) to "apply the brakes" before the kid is overwhelmed, hyperaroused, or dysregulated (Rothschild, 2000).

Activities and Strategies

- Implement school-wide interventions that focus on language-enrichment activities and emphasize teaching social communication and emotional language skills, including emotional labeling, appropriate verbal expressions of emotion, and discussing the causes of one's feelings (Bray, Kehle, Caterino, & Grigerick, 2011).
- Have students list all of the words they can think of to describe emotions. List *sad*, *mad*, and *glad*, and then generate more terms to show extremes or variations of each. Keep a running list.
- Give the students cards with exotic emotion vocabulary, and have them match the cards to basic emotions they are familiar with (e.g., joy, surprise, pride, exasperation, sorrow, worry, delight, contentment).
- Give points for using other than the usual terms.
- Institute periodic emotion check-ins. Ask, "How are you feeling?" and give points for participation and extra points for new descriptors.
- Have kids collect data on emotions they experience during the day, either periodically or at potentially problematic times, such as during transitions, tests, or performance situations.
- Have kids identify times they had experienced strong emotions and had managed well. Help them explore how they were able to do that and how they might be able to do that again in the future.
- Teach students to make "I Statements." These statements help kids express the feeling and say what they need from others without blame or accusations.
- Help students build their emotion vocabulary so they have words to express the level of emotion they are feeling.
- Identify supports for coping that are available in the environment to help with a student's different levels of need.

SKILL UNIT 2: Leave the Bad Stuff by the Door

Targeted Skill:
Expresses emotions verbally.

Materials:
Leave the Bad Stuff by the Door checklist, Leave the Bad Stuff by the Door note

Why

Some students walk in the door upset or angry and ready to create a problem. Experienced educators can read these students' facial expressions and body language and can tell immediately, even before the student speaks, that something is wrong. Adults in a school setting cannot undo what happens to students at home, with friends, in the community, or on the way to school, but adults who recognize that a student is upset may be able to defuse the situation before something goes wrong. This type of preventive action is often more effective than responding *after* a student has lost control. The "Leave the Bad Stuff by the Door" strategy will help students identify things that are upsetting and keep them from becoming dysregulated and therefore able to stay in an instructional setting.

How

The person who implements the "Leave the Bad Stuff by the Door" strategy must have a calm and secure relationship with the student. If not, the student may take out his or her anger, hurt, resentment, sadness, or fear on that person, regardless of the purpose of the interaction. So, the first step is to find an adult who can communicate and interact positively and effectively with the student. The steps are not difficult if the student has a calm, secure relationship with the adult, but progress may take time.

1. First, the adult and student should work together to create a schedule stating where the student will go and what he or she will do at the beginning of each school day. The schedule should require the student to check in with the adult immediately after getting off the bus. (The procedure should be cleared in advance with the teacher or administrator in charge to prevent scheduling conflicts.)

2. Check-ins do not have to be formal or time-consuming. A simple "Hi. How are you today? Is everything okay?" type of conversation will allow the adult to assess the student's demeanor, attitude, and mood. As long as the student seems positive and ready to start the school day, the meeting can remain short. But, on days when the student is clearly agitated, upset, angry, fearful, or unhappy, the adult should discover the problem, find out why the student is upset, and figure out whether the studnt can leave those emotions behind and still have a good day. The adult could have a Leave the Bad Stuff

Here box, like the one shown in the illustration, and use the Leave the Bad Stuff by the Door card to help the student take these steps:
- Articulate what is wrong.
- Ask for help to deal with the problem.
- Calm down enough to start the day.
- Put the *stuff* (the bad feelings from outside school) in the Bad Stuff box by the door.

3. If the student can complete these steps, and the adult is confident that the student is calm enough to go to class, then he or she can let the student go, though checking in on the student during the school day.
4. After the check-in, if the student is still too upset to participate positively in class, additional calm-down procedures should be implemented (e.g., asking the student to begin his or her work in a quiet, calm setting).
5. If possible, the student should return for an end-of-day check-in. If the student had a good day, despite the rough beginning, congratulations are in order!

Scaling Technique

Scaling can help the student think specifically about the present and also be used to send the message that measurable progress is expected. Scaling questions can be framed in a number of ways. The basic format is, "On a scale of 1 to 10, with 1 being the worst this situation could be and 10 being the best the situation could be, what number describes where the situation is today?" During morning check-ins, ask the student to scale or assign a number denoting how he or she is feeling that day. This can effectively give you a quick idea of the student's emotional state and enable you to measure day-to-day progress of the student's ability to manage bad feelings.

Just in Case

Some students are so unaware of the feelings they bring with them to school that it takes them a long time to recognize the role that outside events or people play in affecting their moods. Once students recognize not only how they are feeling but also why they are feeling that way, they may be better able to modify their actions and reactions. Adults working with students who have very stressful home and community situations take on an important role by helping them as they learn how to put aside bad stuff and get through the school day.

BAD STUFF

Leave it here by the door.

Name _____   Date _____

Leave Your Bad Stuff by the Door

What happened before school to make you feel bad? Was it…

- ❏ Trouble with a friend
- ❏ A problem with a family member
- ❏ A situation that happened on the way to school
- ❏ Feelings left over from last night
- ❏ Other: _____

Are you mainly feeling…

- ❏ Angry
- ❏ Hurt
- ❏ Sad
- ❏ Upset/Jumpy
- ❏ Afraid
- ❏ Other: _____

What help do you need, and who can help you? _____
_____

To help you calm down, we will _____

After you are calm, I want you to write your bad feelings on the card and put them in the box by the door. When you walk out of here, the bad stuff needs to stay here so that you have a good day.

Student Name: _____   Adult Name: _____

Date: _____

© 2012 by PRO-ED, Inc.   #13936

Bad Stuff to Leave by the Door

These are the bad feelings I had when I came to school today:

I felt _____

because _____ .

I don't want to ruin my day because of bad stuff that happened outside of school, so I am leaving my bad feelings here, and I am going to try to have a good day.

Student Name: _____

Date: _____

Bad Stuff to Leave by the Door

These are the bad feelings I had when I came to school today:

I felt _____

because _____ .

I don't want to ruin my day because of bad stuff that happened outside of school, so I am leaving my bad feelings here, and I am going to try to have a good day.

Student Name: _____

Date: _____

Skill Unit 3
Accepts criticism and praise

Background Information

"To accept criticism and evaluate one's behavior empowers a student for life."

—Wendy Donahue, *Chicago Tribune* (August 9, 2010)

It is nearly impossible to go through life without facing criticism in some form, and therefore students need to learn how to deal with criticism in healthy, positive ways. They will face criticism at school, in sports, with family and friends, and eventually in a job situation. If kids take criticism too personally, they will allow others to dictate their lives. Kids need to learn that you cannot control or change others; you can only control how you react to them. Kids, like adults, can react to criticism in the following ways: they can ignore it, be motivated by it, reply to it, or let it ruin their positive outlook. Help your students learn how to accept criticism and be motivated by it (Mueller & Dweck, 1998). The best way for your students to deal with criticism is to do the following:

- Listen to what's being said. Don't interrupt to contradict or make excuses.
- Agree with it, when possible.
- Ask questions if you are unsure about anything.
- Admit mistakes and apologize.
- Calmly disagree if it's unfair, by politely saying, "I don't agree with you."

Giving Criticism in a Constructive Way

Teach students how to accept criticism by giving it in a constructive way. This means being calm, not angry, and focusing on the behavior you want to change instead of criticizing the person. It also helps if you can find positive things to say to balance the criticism. Using "I" tends to be less aggressive than using "you." For example, "I noticed you often have good ideas for your group. Sometimes they don't get a chance to share theirs. Do you have ideas about how to improve the situation?"

Giving Praise

Very young students are likely to take praise at face value, but older kids are not. As kids mature, they become aware of possible motives for praising them. If they perceive one to be insincere, they may dismiss the praise. They may also be sensitive to being patronized or manipulated.

Praising kids for their ability makes them focus on looking good rather than on learning. Kids who are praised for their intelligence want to keep proving themselves by doing well, which might sound good, but it's actually counterproductive. In a landmark series of experiments on American fifth-grade students, researchers Claudia Mueller and Carol Dweck (1998) found that kids behaved very differently depending on the kinds of praise they received. Kids who were praised for their intelligence tended to avoid challenges. Instead, they preferred easy tasks. They were also more interested in their competitive standing—how they measured up relative to others—than they were in learning how to improve their future performance. By contrast, kids who were praised for their effort showed the opposite trend. They preferred tasks that were challenging—tasks they could learn from. And kids praised for effort were more interested in learning new strategies for success than they were in finding out how other students had performed.

Kids differed in other respects, too. Compared to kids praised for their effort, kids who were accustomed to being praised for their ability were

- more likely to give up after a failure,
- more likely to perform poorly after a failure, and
- more likely to misrepresent how well they did on a task.

Praising intelligence is not as effective as praising a student's effort and choice of strategies (Henderlong & Lepper, 2002).

Tips

- Praise your student for his or her strategies (e.g., "You found a really good way to do it.").
- Praise your student for specific work (e.g., "You did a great job with those math problems.").
- Praise your student for his persistence or effort (e.g., "I can see you've been practicing." "Your hard work has really paid off.").
- Praising kids for effort (and not innate ability) may help them develop a better mindset for learning.
- Praise kids for traits they have the power to change.
- Avoid praise that compares the student to others.
- Show students how to congratulate others on their successes. They will feel they are coping better as they congratulate others.

Activities and Strategies

- Have the student search on the Internet, in the newspaper, or on television for reviews about a favorite athlete, actor, singer, or writer. Have the student highlight or point out less than flattering statements or criticism. Stress that everyone has to deal with criticism, no matter how popular or admired they are. As an option, have the student investigate further how the celebrity handles criticism (ignores, voices back, motivates) and decide if that approach would work in their situations. Have the student pay attention to instances when and how the celebrity received praise.
- Allow the student to practice taking time to cool off when receiving criticism. One method handling criticism is to refrain from verbally defending yourself and instead walking away and cooling off before reacting. It is human nature to want to respond or defend oneself when criticized. Set up a code word between you and the student. If someone criticizes the student, look at the student and say the code word to signal that he or she should walk away to cool off rather than respond or retaliate.

- Be a role model by ignoring insults or criticisms and staying positive. The next time you are criticized, use it as an opportunity to teach the student by example. For instance, if someone at school criticizes the bulletin board you designed, instead of becoming angry or defensive, ignore the comment and find a positive response, such as, "I like that this display could be done quickly," or "I like to experiment with different designs to see which I like best—it's fun." Continue to model how to keep a positive attitude when you have been criticized.
- Let the student accept constructive criticism from two or three people he or she respects. Encourage your student to mull over the criticism and reflect on what unspoken advice the individuals may have meant by the criticism.
- Based on constructive criticism, guide the student in setting a goal to improve on an activity or behavior. Remind the student that the criticism was meant to motivate them to become a better person by someone who knows they are capable of more.
- Let the student choose an activity or behavior to change what is important to them. The student will be much more successful at using criticism as a motivator if he or she feels in control of making changes or improvements based on the criticism.
- Record the activity or behavior the student is trying to improve so it can be reviewed. Sometimes the best way to acknowledge criticism is to see it first-hand, through someone else's eyes. Sports players do this all the time by reviewing videotapes of their plays with the coach to watch for mistakes and to think about making improvements. If it is a behavior the student was criticized about, try to catch that behavior (temper, impatience, etc.) on camera. Oftentimes, kids do not realize how they look or come across unless they see it themselves.
- Document any improvements from the constructive criticism. Keeping track of improvements based on criticism will validate that constructive criticism can be motivating and have positive outcomes. Point out or show the student videotaped evidence in which he or she used criticism to become better at something. Because students learn best from concrete experiences, document positive changes the student made based on criticism.

SKILL UNIT 3: Just Say Thanks

Targeted Skill:
Accepts criticism and praise.

Materials:
Just Say Thanks cue cards

Why

Students, like adults, have a difficult time accepting criticism. What is surprising is that some students also have trouble accepting praise or compliments. Praise may make some students uncomfortable, but it is important that they learn to acknowledge it graciously. One approach to both praise and criticism is to "Just Say Thanks." If students can thank someone for offering critical feedback, acknowledge that it suggests positive changes, and then move on, the criticism will have been helpful. If the feedback is positive, the student can still say thank you and be happy that someone is appreciative of what he or she has done.

How

Here is a routine adults can teach students to help them accept feedback, whether it is criticism or praise. Like all positive social skills that are new and may be challenging for students to learn, "Just Say Thanks" should be explained, modeled, and practiced. Because all students can use this skill, it could be taught to a whole class, a small group, or to individual students.

1. Explain to students that it can be difficult to accept and respond to both criticism and praise. Provide some examples, and ask students to suggest examples from their own experiences.

   Example of Criticism

   - Your mom and dad are angry with you because you won't stop talking or texting during dinner. They tell you that you are inconsiderate and rude.
   - One of your teachers gets upset because he feels like you didn't try hard enough on an assignment. He says it seems like you don't care.
   - Your best friend yells at you and tells you she wishes you would talk less and listen more and suggests that you are selfish.

   Example of Praise

   - You do great on a test, and your teacher tells everybody in the class how well you did.
   - Your parents brag to your grandparents about how nice you were to take care of your little sister.

- A new student in school thanks you for helping him out and for being nice to him when he didn't know anybody else.
2. Make sure all of your students have a chance to share at least one example of criticism and one example of praise.
3. Explain to the students that not all criticism is justified and not all praise is deserved. People sometimes get blamed for things that were not their fault, or singled out for praise they don't deserve. Because not all feedback is deserved or even fair, it can be hard to accept.
4. Suggest that there are many ways to deal with criticism or praise, but that one technique to start with is very simple: "Just Say Thanks." After mastering this response, students can add other steps that might help, but, at first, just saying thanks is a direct and clear way to deal with the situation. It often defuses criticism and lets others know that they are not going to be defensive or get angry.
5. Model for students how to say thanks without looking disrespectful, being sarcastic, or showing embarrassment. To say thanks to praise or criticism, students can respond as follows:
   - Look at the person who is talking.
   - Nod and make eye contact.
   - Say a simple phrase such as, "Thanks for telling me." "I appreciate the feedback. Thanks." "Thank you for letting me know what you think. I will consider it."
6. Ask students to practice saying thanks, even when it is difficult or stressful to do so. To help them remember to say thanks in challenging, real-life situations, students can keep a cue card readily available. They can refer to the cue card several times a day and practice saying thanks.

Just in Case

Recognize that students may encounter others who are abusive, unfair, or mean-spirited. Accepting criticism or praise is not the same as accepting abusive treatment. Make sure you help students understand what they can do when they have received verbal or physical abuse.

Just saying thanks is a beginning step for many students. They will also need to learn additional strategies when given feedback. After mastering this beginning step, they can learn to express a complaint, suggest compromises, and develop personal plans for improvement. All of these skills will complement their initial step of saying thanks.

You may not want to hear it, but listen, and then **Just Say *Thanks*.**	You may not want to hear it, but listen, and then **Just Say *Thanks*.**
You may not want to hear it, but listen, and then **Just Say *Thanks*.**	You may not want to hear it, but listen, and then **Just Say *Thanks*.**
You may not want to hear it, but listen, and then **Just Say *Thanks*.**	You may not want to hear it, but listen, and then **Just Say *Thanks*.**
You may not want to hear it, but listen, and then **Just Say *Thanks*.**	You may not want to hear it, but listen, and then **Just Say *Thanks*.**

© 2012 by PRO-ED, Inc.   #13936

Skill Unit 4
Takes responsibility for actions

Background Information

Taking responsibility for one's actions and oneself is a prized characteristic. Self-discipline reflects internalization, which is defined as "taking over the values and attitudes of society as one's own so that socially acceptable behavior is motivated not by anticipation of external consequences but by intrinsic or internal factors" (Grusec & Goodnow, 1994, p. 4). Self-discipline entails determining and choosing right from wrong and knowing that behaving in the right way does not necessarily lead to external rewards or avoidance of punishment. The ultimate indicator of the effectiveness of classroom discipline (and school-wide discipline) is not how many students are referred to the office or how well students behave under close adult supervision but the extent to which students act responsibly when supervision is minimal and when external rewards and punishment are not a factor.

Research shows that self-discipline promotes positive relations with others and a positive school climate, fosters academic achievement, and promotes self-worth and emotional well-being (Bear, Manning, & Izard, 2003). Social and emotional learning (SEL) is a national initiative in education that focuses on promoting social and emotional competencies associated with self-discipline. SEL programs target five key competencies: self-awareness, social awareness, responsible decision making, self-management, and relationship skills, also known as the CASEL skills (see the Collaborative for Academic, Social, and Emotional Learning website at www.CASEL.org).

Activities and Strategies

- Infuse lessons and activities for developing self-discipline into the existing social studies, literacy, and health education curriculum. Perspective-taking and responsible decision-making examples can be found in many areas of the curriculum.
- Include multiple models of targeted behaviors, social cognitions, and emotions in the school's curriculum and in the real life of the classroom and school. Include models by teachers, staff, and students as well as models in literature, history, sports, and the media. Modeling behaviors such as social problem solving and moral decision making is the most efficient method of instruction (Bear, 2011). Modeling shows students the appropriate ways to think and act, motivates them to engage in the behavior observed, helps develop values and standards that underlie the behaviors observed, and triggers emotional reactions observed in others (Bandura, 1986).
- Provide opportunities for students to apply social and moral problem-solving skills and responsible behavior, including class meetings, programs and activities for conflict resolution, peer mediation, service learning, cooperative learning, and sports and extracurricular activities.

- Confront excuses tactfully, and highlight models of desired thinking, feeling, and acting. Children tend to excuse or justify moral transgressions with rationalizations (e.g., "He started it." "I didn't mean to hurt him." "Others did it, too.").
- Teach a problem-solving model that is appropriate for the students' age, and then have them use it to come to a decision. They can use this structure to support the responsible nature of their decision and their actions.

SKILL UNIT 4: Please Check Me Out

Targeted Skill:
Takes responsibility for actions.

Materials:
Please Check Me Out Contract, Please Check Me Out Consequences forms

Why

Some behaviors are nonnegotiable. Possessing, using, or bringing a weapon to school is one of those nonnegotiable behaviors. If a student who had previously brought or used a weapon in school returns to school, then strict, intensive measures should be taken to ensure that the offending student never repeats the behavior. Administrators should have tight, enforceable guidelines and procedures in place to prevent such behavior.

It is also a good idea for the student to participate in a voluntary program that allows for regular and random checks of his or her locker, backpack, clothing, and other property. The checks can be used as part of a comprehensive strategy that includes teaching the student to make good choices and ensuring that the student takes responsibility for his or her actions and consents to the checks. The "Please Check Me Out" strategy includes such voluntary checks. There are legal guidelines and procedures established by federal, state, and local entities that must be implemented when weapons are brought to school. This strategy is not intended to circumvent those guidelines and procedures. We strongly recommend that school personnel ask their legal representatives to review and approve this strategy before implementing it.

How

This strategy should be implemented by a campus administrator—someone who has the authority to make quick decisions about school rules, their application, and the consequences related to those rules. To implement the idea, take the following steps:

1. **Meet with the student, and outline the rules and expectations.**
   When a student returns after being removed and punished for bringing a weapon to school, the student and his or her parents or guardians should meet with a campus administrator. In that meeting, the administrator should explain the district and campus policies regarding the possession of weapons. In addition, if possible, the school district resource officer or local police should attend the meeting and explain the legal consequences of weapon possession. Finally, if the student has a disability and is served in special education or under Section 504 of the Vocational Rehabilitation Act, a representative from that program should attend. At this meeting, specific rules, behavioral expectations, and consequences should be explained to the student.

2. **Establish a voluntary check-in program with the student.**
    If students must pass through metal detectors or are subject to electronic monitoring and searches when entering school, explain the procedures, demonstrate them, and conduct a practice session with the student. In addition, all parties should sign legal forms, including releases, IEP committee paperwork, and other required documents. This strategy is not intended to address physical searches of a student. All legal guidelines should be followed by school personnel regarding physical searches.
3. **Establish *voluntary* procedures with the student and his or her parents or guardians that will allow daily and random checks.**
    The student and his or her parents or guardians will work with the campus administrator to create a contract in which the student will voluntarily allow him- or herself and his or her lockers, desks, and other property to be searched. The contract would not take the place of any required campus procedures. The purpose of the contract is for the student to take responsibility for his or her actions. Ensure that all parties understand the contract and consequences, and set up a "Please Check Me Out" schedule. Also, share information about a random schedule of checks.
4. **Discuss with the student the relationship between voluntary checks and trust of school personnel.**
    There is no guarantee that a student who has brought a weapon to school will ever again be fully trusted by school personnel. However, because the student has returned to campus, it is important for them to work with the student. Discussions with the student should emphasize the positive effects of agreeing to the checks, cooperating with adults, and adopting an attitude that conveys that the student has nothing to hide and has changed. Over time, if the student effectively demonstrates positive behavior and the checks occur without any infractions, trust may be rebuilt.
5. **After agreeing to the contract, agree to the consequences.**
    The Please Check Me Out Consequences should be selected and agreed to by both the administrator and the student. These consequences focus on social approval and responsibilities, and by having the student focus on positive outcomes associated with taking responsibility for his or her actions, it is hoped that the student will begin to recognize and appreciate not just the tangible rewards but also the positive feelings that come with personal responsibility.

Just in Case

It is important that the student agrees to the contract, expresses a desire to participate, and volunteers to abide by the contract's requirements. The contract should not be used as punishment, because it would eliminate the voluntary aspect in which the student takes responsibility for his or her actions.

Please Check Me Out Contract

Student Name: _____

I agree to allow both regular daily and random checks of my personal items, lockers, desks, and any other items used by me while in school.

I also agree to allow checks of _____.

I want to do this because:

_____

_____

I understand that there will be disciplinary and legal consequences if I bring or use a weapon again.

I also understand that there will be positive consequences if I do not bring or use a weapon again. These are listed on the attached form.

Student Signature _____ Date _____

Administrator Name: _____

I agree to conduct both regular daily and random checks of _____'s personal items, lockers, desks, and any other items used while in school.

I also agree to conduct checks of _____.

I understand that he/she is doing this voluntarily.

I understand that there will be disciplinary and legal consequences if he/she brings or uses a weapon again.

I also understand that there will be some positive consequences if he/she does not bring or use a weapon again. These are listed on the attached form.

I also agree to communicate daily/weekly with _____'s parents or guardians.

Administrator Signature _____ Date _____

Parent/Guardian Name: _____

I agree to allow both regular daily and random checks of _____'s personal items, lockers, desks, and any other items used while in school.

I also agree to conduct checks of _____.

I understand that he/she is doing this voluntarily.

I understand that there will be disciplinary and legal consequences if he/she brings or uses a weapon again.

I also understand that there will be some positive consequences if he/she does not bring or use a weapon again. These are listed on the attached form.

Parent/Guardian Signature _____ Date _____

© 2012 by PRO-ED, Inc.   #13936

Name _____ Date _____

Please Check Me Out Consequences

The positive consequences for abiding by this contract are provided here. It is understood that any violation of rules and laws related to weapons in school will result in punishment as prescribed by federal, state, and local rules and laws. This contract is designed for use from _____ to _____.

The following consequences will occur:

0 infractions after 3 weeks:
- ❏ Phone call to parents or guardian
- ❏ Lunch meeting with administrator
- ❏ Other: _____

0 infractions after 6 weeks:
- ❏ Phone call to parents or guardian
- ❏ Lunch meeting with administrator
- ❏ Other: _____

0 infractions after 9 weeks:
- ❏ Phone call to parents or guardian
- ❏ Lunch meeting with administrator
- ❏ Other: _____

0 infractions after 12 weeks:
- ❏ Phone call to parents or guardian
- ❏ Lunch meeting with administrator
- ❏ Responsibility on campus (_____)
- ❏ Other: _____
- ❏ Other: _____

0 infractions after 15 weeks:
- ❏ Phone call to parents or guardian
- ❏ Lunch meeting with administrator
- ❏ Responsibility on campus (_____)
- ❏ Other: _____
- ❏ Other: _____

0 infractions after 18 weeks:
- ❏ Phone call to parents or guardian
- ❏ Lunch meeting with administrator
- ❏ Responsibility on campus (_____)
- ❏ Other: _____
- ❏ Other: _____

Student initials: _____ Date: _____

Administrator initials: _____ Date: _____

Parent/Guardian initials: _____ Date: _____

© 2012 by PRO-ED, Inc.   #13936

SKILL UNIT 4: Just Say Yes

Targeted Skill:
Takes responsibility for actions.

Materials:
"Just Say Yes" Cue Cards, Brainstorming List

When a student fails to take responsibility for his or her behavior, adults often find it more upsetting than if the student admitted fault and took responsibility for the action. Students who refuse to take responsibility for their behavior can escalate adults' reactions to the behavior and make the situation worse. In addition, students who fail to take responsibility for their actions may not believe that they have a problem or that they have done anything wrong. For individuals who do not see and admit their responsibility, changing the behavior is more difficult.

How

"Just Say Yes" is a first step to helping students with the difficult step of taking responsibility. It is not the only step that students should take, but it may help deescalate a situation and prevent blow-ups and overreactions. Teachers, counselors, and administrators can use this strategy with one student, a small group, or with a whole class. It can be adapted for any age group. Here is how to use the "Just Say Yes" activity.

1. Explain to the student why it is important to take responsibility for one's own actions, and, using the Brainstorming Form, ask the student to suggest some of his or her own reasons why. Reasons for taking responsibility might include the following:
    - If you admit that you were wrong, people don't stay mad at you.
    - If you take responsibility, you can deal with the problem and get it over with more quickly.
    - If you tell the truth, people will trust you.
    - If you take responsibility, other people will believe you, even if they don't like what you did.

2. Show the student the three-step script on the cue cards. This simple, three-sentence script is very direct and, hopefully, effective. However, teachers and counselors can write scripts with students that fit the student's age, style of speech, and comfort level. Explain to the student: "If you do something wrong or you break a rule, you can say these three things. Most of the time, this will keep you from getting in more trouble. If you take responsibility this way, you may also feel like you are not embarrassed. Here's what you can say:
    - Yes, I did it.
    - I'm sorry.
    - I would like to explain and answer your questions.

3. Teach the student to follow these three simple steps by modeling the language for them. Be sure you model body language as well. If you like, you can change the words, but keep them simple and direct so that the student remembers them.
4. Practice using the "Just Say Yes" script. Here are some examples of scenarios that you can use for practice. These scenarios are for a variety of ages, so rewrite or create more to fit your students. After an adult explains the scenarios, the student can practice just saying yes until the actions and words start to come naturally.
    * You are fooling around in the hall and are late for class. The teacher says, "Well, surprise, surprise, you're late again." You should say, "_____."
    * Your friend Ashley talks you into taking another girl's PE clothes, who then gets in trouble for not dressing out. The girl sees you when you try to put the clothes back in her locker and tells the teacher. When the teacher confronts you, you should say, "_____."
    * You are mad at Ronald because he called you a name, so you curse at him and call him a worse name. The teacher doesn't hear Ronald, she just hears you. You get sent to the office. You should say, "_____."
    * Jaime tripped you on the way to recess. You punch him, and Mr. Jones sees you. When Mr. Jones yells at you, you should say, "_____."
5. To help students actually *use* the "Just Say Yes" strategy, give them cue cards that have the steps written on them. Ask students to keep the cards somewhere visible. For young students, this might be on the corner of their desk. Older students can keep the cards in their notebook or in a pocket.

The adult's calm approach is critical here! When an adult thinks a student has done something wrong, it is important that he or she talk to the student calmly. Taking a moment to calm oneself and reregulate helps the adult prevent an escalated incident. Of course, adults should determine what happened in difficult situations, but asking first, rather than accusing, will help keep the situation under control. Remember, our calm begets their calm.

Remember, too, that sometimes a student may *not* have done anything wrong. It is always better to gather information first before jumping to a conclusion. You can also teach students a simple script to use when they really did not do anything wrong (e.g., "No, I did not _____. I will be happy to tell you what happened, where I was, and what I was doing.").

"Just Say Yes" Cue Cards

---

① Yes, I did it.

② I'm Sorry.

③ I would like to explain and answer your questions.

---

① Yes, I did it.

② I'm Sorry.

③ I would like to explain and answer your questions.

---

① Yes, I did it.

② I'm Sorry.

③ I want to explain.

---

① Yes, I did it.

② I'm Sorry.

③ I want to explain.

© 2012 by PRO-ED, Inc.   #13936

Name _____ Date _____

Brainstorming List

It's Good to Take Responsibility Because:

1.
2.
3.
4.
5.
6.
7.
8.
9.
10.
11.
12.
13.
14.
15.
16.
17.
18.
19.
20.

Skill Unit 5
Initiates a calming strategy after being upset

Background Information

Stress is the body's reaction to any situation that is perceived as being an emergency. It is not the events or circumstances themselves but rather the body's reactions to them. It is helpful for students to have inner mechanisms available that reduce the body's stress reaction. Here are some benefits:

- Increased self-awareness and self-understanding
- Greater ability to relax the body and release physical tension
- Improved concentration and ability to pay attention, which is crucial to learning
- The ability to deal with stressful situations more effectively by creating a more relaxed way of responding to stressors
- Greater control over thoughts, with less domination by unwelcome thoughts

Students can draw upon their internal and external resources to build their repertoire of calming strategies. The following are lists of internal and external resources adapted from suggestions by Rothschild (2000, 2003), Ogden et al. (2006), and Levine and Kline (2007).

Examples of Internal Resources

- The capacities to ground and the use of mindfulness to observe sensations of dysregulation and not act on them
- Somatic memory of sensation that is experienced as stimulating, calming, soothing, or comforting and that can be used in problematic situations to maintain emotional regulation
- Using body awareness to anchor, gauge arousal, apply the brakes to maintain emotional regulation, or to shift from dysregulation
- Abilities, unique skills, talents, and interests such as verbal or math skills, artistic ability, leadership skills, athletic ability, and other nonverbal abilities
- Physical abilities such as sight, hearing, smell, touch, large or small motor agility and balance, a healthy body, and energy
- Personality qualities such as initiative, generosity, kindness toward others, dependability, a sense of humor, and the ability to make and keep friends
- Action that is experienced as establishing personal boundaries and having the strength to defend oneself
- The ability to ask for help

Examples of External Resources

- Caring and involved parents
- Adults who can be depended upon, including teachers, counselors, and members of the school staff

- Extended nurturing family, friends, pets, and a larger community of people and activities such as coaches, scout leaders and cultural, social, athletic, and religious opportunities
- Access and opportunities to experience the natural environment
- Access to an environment enriched with books, art supplies, toys, and music
- Objects and other experiences that offer either stimulation or calming, soothing comfort for the senses such as, music, color, textured materials, soft blankets, and stuffed animals

Activities and Strategies

- Teach students to ground with the following or a similar exercise: **Breathe in slowly. Breathe out slowly. Breathe in. Breathe out. Notice how your feet make contact with the ground. Breathe in slowly and breathe out slowly. Imagine that you have roots growing from the soles of your feet stretching deep into the earth. Even if you are on the top floor of a building or on a jet 30,000 feet up, imagine your roots grounding you. Think about the quiet power of these roots. Feel yourself firmly planted, flexible yet strong against the wind. Notice and continue to feel the connection to the ground with each inhale and exhale.**
- Help kids to stop and observe their somatic experience (what's going on inside their bodies) at the first sign of dysregulation. This mindful awareness helps them shift from focusing on what they believe is the source of their distress. Practice learning this skill with everyday activities such as washing hands or eating.
- Once kids can focus on what is going on inside their bodies, they are ready to learn tracking sensation, a range of interventions using somatic experience. Sensations are physiological happenings in the body that are not associated with thoughts. Sensations offer important information about current arousal and emotional state. When there is potential for becoming dysregulated, mindful awareness makes it possible to observe sensations and then to engage the upper cognitive areas of the brain to make decisions (Fisher & Ogden, 2009). The sensations of hyperarousal can become signals for a student to slow down and think, making it possible to master situations that previously caused trouble. Practice observing the sensations such as pressure, temperature change on the skin, vibrations, warmth, racing heart, jitters, nausea, hunger, muscle tension, dizziness, and feeling energetic or tired.
- Interrupt strong expressions of emotion, and direct the student's attention back to the sensations in his or her body. For example, if a student begins to experience strong emotion, giving him the instruction to put aside the fear, anger, or whatever the emotion is and begin to identify and notice the sensations.

SKILL UNIT 5: Three Cards for Calming

Targeted Skill:
Initiates a calming strategy after being upset.

Materials:
Calming Cards

Why

This idea provides students with a mechanism to gain some time to think about what they want to do about an upsetting incident. The prompts support waiting to take action, focus on their calming strategy, and observe what they did that was successful.

How

Practice with minor situations so that students can become familiar with the steps. The cards can be displayed on the student's desk or kept in a pocket. The boxes can be prefilled with the student's ideas of options or can be left blank.

Example

Later, I choose to . . .	Now I need to . . .	What worked for me . . .
■ Write or draw about what happened ■ Tell a helpful adult ■ Make a plan to prevent this again	■ Ground myself and take several slow breaths ■ Notice the sensation in my body ■ Track the sensation as it moves through my body	■ Grounding ■ Knowing I could go to Ms. Jones for help

Later, I choose to . . .	Now I need to . . .	What worked for me . . .

Later, I choose to . . .	Now I need to . . .	What worked for me . . .

Later, I choose to . . .	Now I need to . . .	What worked for me . . .

Later, I choose to . . .	Now I need to . . .	What worked for me . . .

SKILL UNIT 5

The Keep Calm Activity

Targeted Skill:

Initiates a calming strategy after being upset.

Materials:

Keep Calm Poster

Why

This simple, four-step breathing activity comes from the book *Emotionally Intelligent Parenting* (Elias, Tobias, & Friedlander, 1999). It can be used whenever the student is upset or self-control is needed. Teach these four simple steps to your student (and try it yourself!).

How

Post these steps in a quiet corner or other place in the classroom or office as a reminder.

1. Stop and take a look around.
2. Tell yourself, "Keep calm."
3. Take a deep breath through your nose while you count to five, hold it while you count to two, and then breathe out through your mouth while you count to five.
4. Repeat these steps until you feel calm.

Keep Calm

1 Stop and take a look around.

2 Tell yourself, "Keep calm."

3 Take a deep breath through your nose while you count to five, hold it while you count to two, and then breathe out through your mouth while you count to five.

4 Repeat these steps until you feel calm.

SKILL UNIT 5: Getting Calm Feels Great

Targeted Skill:
Initiates a calming strategy after being upset.

Materials:
Getting Calm Feels Great Plan form; I Need a Break card; Secret Signals; Yay, Me! card

Why

School can be a stressful for both adults and students, and so it is important that everyone know and use strategies that will help them calm down when they are agitated or upset. Here are some easy-to-follow steps that you can teach students who need to learn these skills. But, it is important to provide opportunities for students to practice these skills after learning them. Modeling or practicing only once in a while is not enough for students to master the skills well enough to use them automatically.

How

1. Teach the student to recognize when he or she is becoming upset. This includes identifying the situations (triggers) that cause the agitation and recognizing the physical sensations that result. Common triggers that result in students getting upset include the following:
   * Difficult assignments
   * Teasing
   * Being called names
   * Problems at home, on the bus, or with a friend outside of school
   * Worry
   * Illness
   * Constant nettling by others
   * Nervousness or embarrassment
   * Guilt
   * Others: _____

2. After identifying these possible triggers, ask students to suggest other situations, people, or problems that cause them to get upset and write this information in the first section of the Getting Calm Feels Great Plan. For younger students, include photographs of the situations mentioned. Common physical sensations that indicate one is getting upset include the following:
   * Tight shoulders, neck, or face
   * Tensing hands or clenching fists
   * Red neck and/or face; feeling hot
   * Feel like crying
   * Want to hit or throw something
   * Just want to get away
   * Can't look anyone in the eyes

- Pacing or walking very fast
- Feel like cursing or yelling
- Others: _____

3. Work with students to generate a list of techniques they can use to calm down. Each student should develop his or her own personal strategy, but here are some effective options:
   - Deep breathing
   - Count to 10, backwards and forwards
   - Put your head down and close your eyes
   - Put on earphones and listen to quiet music
   - Take a water or bathroom break (with permission)
   - Show the teacher an I Need a Break card, and move to the break area
   - Play a slide show in your mind of things you like; visualize
   - Repeat a calming phrase
   - Others: _____

4. Teach your students how to recognize when they are calm. One simple way to do this is to discuss feelings that are opposite of those described in Step 2. For example, if they felt like crying before and now they don't, they are probably getting calmer. Help students be very specific in both Steps 2 and 4 so that they are clear about what they are feeling and what it means.

5. Discuss with students some ways that they can celebrate when they are able to calm themselves down. Calming themselves is a big deal for students, and they need to appreciate their success. Students do not need to celebrate publicly but can recognize their own progress and use a personal method of congratulating themselves. Here are some simple steps they can take on their own:
   - Write themselves a note
   - Use a signal that only the student and teacher know, such as a special wave, a wink, or a thumbs-up sign
   - Keep a small bead on a string in their notebook or desk (no one needs to know what the bead represents)
   - Keep a journal and write about their success
   - Draw a picture of themselves doing well or a picture that represents how they feel, and include it in their journal
   - Call their parent or grandparent and share their success
   - Others: _____

6. Make sure the student practices his or her plan when he or she is calm, and document the practice time on the bottom of the plan.

Name _____ Date _____

Getting Calm Feels Great Plan

These things make me feel upset:

When _____

_____

_____

_____

_____

_____

I can tell I am starting to get upset because:

I feel _____

_____

_____

_____

_____

_____

Before or after I get upset, I can calm myself:

I will do these things:

1. _____

2. _____

3. _____

I will know that I am calm when:

_____

I will celebrate by:

_____

I practiced on: _____ _____ _____

_____ _____ _____

© 2012 by PRO-ED, Inc.   #13936

I need a break.	I need a break.
Yay, me! I got calm when I was upset.	Yay, me! I got calm when I was upset.
I need a break.	I need a break.
Yay, me! I got calm when I was upset.	Yay, me! I got calm when I was upset.

SKILL UNIT 5: Cross Off the Days

Targeted Skill:

Initiates a calming strategy after being upset.

Materials:

Aggression: What Is It?; Cross Off the Days Goal and Calendar; Choose This, Not That forms

Why

People who set goals to change their own behavior recognize the value of self-monitoring and self-reinforcement. Monitoring oneself does not have to be complicated or time-consuming. "Cross Off the Days" is a simple activity that students of any age can use on their own to help them reduce verbal and physical aggression, especially when others provoke them.

The best goals are significant (relevant and important to the student), specific (clear, concrete, and observable), small (reasonable and attainable), start-based (the presence or start of something desirable), and self-manageable (within the student's control) (Murphy, 2008). Although adults can help the student set a goal, provide feedback and positive reinforcement, and reward the student when the goal is met, the student is responsible for evaluating, monitoring, and recording his or her own behavior.

How

To help the student implement this strategy, take the following steps:

1. Work with the student to identify specific behaviors that are considered by others to be verbally or physically aggressive. Use the Aggression: What Is It? chart to guide the discussion. Be clear about what is considered verbal or physical aggression, and discuss examples of the student's past behavior that may be misinterpreted by others.
2. Work with the student to list nonaggressive ways to respond to situations, and give this set of nonaggressive responses a name (e.g., Cool Responding, Assertiveness, Cool Headedness).
3. Ask the student to set a goal for increasing a nonaggressive response. Using a scale from 1 to 10, where 10 describes the ideal goal, ask the student to establish his or her current location on the scale and describe what that looks like in terms of handling a situation with a cool head. For example: **My goal is to use respectful words to tell a person what I need. A 10 would be when I do this 100% of the time. Today I am at a 5 because I am doing these things right now but still having some difficulties. I plan to move to a 6. When I'm at a 6, I'll be doing** _____.
4. Use the Cross off the Days Goal and Calendar form to record the student's goal and daily scaling, and require the student to check in each day and share his or her progress.

5. Work with the student to identify triggers that cause anger and some acceptable responses to them by identifying upsetting events, individuals with whom the student has a negative history, or outside stressors that might cause an aggressive reaction. Have the student write some alternatives to aggression on the Choose This, Not That cards. Coaching students in ways to respond when provoked will require close monitoring and regular feedback. Praise the student when he or she handles a challenging situation well.

Just in Case

Personality clashes are common and can happen in school, just as they happen in families and in the workplace. If an aggressive student has a particular problem with specific individuals in school, consider how to minimize the likelihood of an explosive or negative situation between the two. This may involve having them stay away from each other, using a third party to resolve disputes, or planning ahead to teach the student how best to communicate with the other person.

Name _____   Date _____

Aggression: What Is It?

AGGRESSIVE	ACCEPTABLE RESPONSES
Verbal	
Physical	

Name _____   Date _____

Cross Off the Days Goal and Calendar

My goal is to increase my ability to _____.

I will circle my scale number towards my goal on this calendar.

When I meet my goal, I will earn _____.

The adult who is working to help me meet this goal is _____.

	WHERE ARE YOU TODAY ON THE SCALE?
SCALE	10 9 8 7 6 5 4 3 2 1
	1 2 3 4 5 6 7 8 9 10 11 12 13 14 15
	Day

© 2012 by PRO-ED, Inc.   #13936

Choose This, Not That
⊕ If someone teases me, I will
_____.
🚫 I won't
_____.

Choose This, Not That
⊕ If someone calls me a name, I will
_____.
🚫 I won't
_____.

Choose This, Not That
⊕ If someone takes my stuff, I will
_____.
🚫 I won't
_____.

Choose This, Not That
⊕ If someone yells at me, I will
_____.
🚫 I won't
_____.

Choose This, Not That
⊕ If someone accuses me of something I didn't do, I will
_____.
🚫 I won't
_____.

Choose This, Not That
⊕ If someone _____, I will
_____.
🚫 I won't
_____.

Choose This, Not That
⊕ If someone accuses me of something I didn't do, I will
_____.
🚫 I won't
_____.

Choose This, Not That
⊕ If someone _____, I will
_____.
🚫 I won't
_____.

© 2012 by PRO-ED, Inc.   #13936

Skill Unit 6
Follows directions from adults

Background Information

Learning to follow directions is an important life skill. Few things are more frustrating or infuriating as having students ignore instructions. But how do teachers convince students that it is important to follow directions—not just to please them or avoid punishments, but to make the students' own lives easier? After all, a child's health and safety can depend on his or her ability to follow directions. Kids function better in school, sports, and other group activities when they know how to carry out instructions.

Activities and Strategies

- Throughout the school, explicitly teach and actively acknowledge how to follow directions from adults. This level of educational support requires the active participation of all staff, including teachers, administrators, paraprofessionals, cafeteria workers, playground supervisors, bus drivers, and other support staff.
- Teach positively stated expectations along with the routines and behaviors that actively demonstrate those expectations. The explicit teaching of routines will benefit all students while also providing important opportunities for the rehearsal of positive behaviors for students with difficulties (DuPaul, Stoner, & O'Reilly, 2011).
- Use a school-wide or classroom acknowledgement system to implement an expectation.
- Provide students with cues, prompts, or signals that function as reminders to follow directions from adults.
- Take time to identify individual students' predictable problems with following directions. This allows the teacher to precorrect the behaviors before they occur, thus increasing student success.
- Make instructions easy to understand. Make sure directions are specific and not open to misinterpretation.
- Give choices—not commands. Whenever possible, let students decide how or when to follow directions. Be careful, however, to avoid using words implying that *not* doing the task is one of the options.
- Catch the kid being good. Reinforce the student at least three times for every one negative correction. Praise for effort. Credit the student with making the expected behavior happen.
- Ask the student to repeat your request. Getting the student to recite rules and instructions out loud can prevent protests of "I didn't know" or "I didn't understand" later on. Ask young, easily distracted kids to repeat your directions silently several times. Offer

older kids a written checklist or, better yet, have them write down the information themselves.
- Implement behavioral self-management using self-recording (student records the frequency of the specific behavior on a data sheet), self-evaluation (student self-records the behavior and evaluates the behavior against a specific criterion), or self-reinforcement (student self-records, self-evaluates, and self-reinforces) (Bear, 2011).

SKILL UNIT 6: Say OK, Get a Ticket

Targeted Skill:
Follows directions from adults.

Materials:
OK Tickets, OK Menu

Why

When students refuse to follow adults' directions, it is often a sign of a general lack of compliance. Noncompliance, in turn, can indicate a lack of respect for authority and an antisocial attitude. Very few things upset adults more than students who refuse to comply with requests and follow directions. In addition, when an adult tries to enforce direction-following, the conflict between the adult and the student may escalate to a serious situation, and even to a physical altercation.

How

Teaching students who are generally noncompliant to change their habits and to cooperate and follow directions will likely take time. Some students are extremely oppositional and will refuse to do anything an adult asks them to do. It is important to begin the process, though, and the younger the student, the better. When the student learns to respect adult authority and follow adults' directions, everyone in school will be happier and more comfortable.

Here is a strategy that can be used to teach compliance and direction-following. It is not the only method of improving students' compliance, but it is a good way to start. Here's how "Say OK, Get a Ticket" works:

1. This strategy will be most effective if it is used consistently. First, have a team meeting and share information about how "Say OK, Get a Ticket" will work. One adult on the team should agree to coordinate the approach, meeting with the student at the beginning and end of each school day. At the beginning of the day, the adult should explain to the student how the plan works:
   - Each time an adult gives the student a direction and he or she follows it after only one or two requests, the adult will give the student a ticket.
   - The tickets can be exchanged for privileges or items of interest to the student from the OK Menu. Examples for young students include a pizza lunch with the teacher, a phone call to Mom, or a new set of colored pencils. Examples of items for older students include MP3 cards, art supplies, or a coupon for a special lunch. The adults and the student will need to work together to agree on the items on the OK Menu as well as how many tickets are required for each item.

2. Every morning, the adult will remind the student what he or she needs to do (follow directions) and what he or she will earn (tickets, privileges). It is important that the adult follow through with this morning meeting.
3. At the end of the day, the adult should again meet with the student to see how many tickets he or she has earned. This processing time is very important, not only to count the tickets but also to problem solve and discuss why the student did or did not earn tickets. Tickets can be saved until the student has enough for a valuable item on the OK Menu. Again, the adult should discuss the student's progress with him or her, provide feedback and praise, and problem solve. If the student has difficulty with a specific adult, then the student will need to learn how to avoid conflict, express his or her concerns to the adult, or follow directions.

Just in Case

This strategy is a beginning step to use with a noncompliant student. Of course, adults should explain the intangible benefits of cooperating and following directions at school (e.g., the student will do better in school and be happier because he or she is not in trouble all the time). However, it is important to start somewhere, and a reward-based system can be both necessary and effective.

OK Tickets

You said "OK" and you did OK. Good for you.	You said "OK" and you did OK. Good for you.
You said "OK" and you did OK. Good for you.	You said "OK" and you did OK. Good for you.
You said "OK" and you did OK. Good for you.	You said "OK" and you did OK. Good for you.
You said "OK" and you did OK. Good for you.	You said "OK" and you did OK. Good for you.

OK Menu

TICKETS

❶ _____

❷ _____

❸ _____

❹ _____

❺ _____

❻ _____

SKILL UNIT 6: I'll Say It, You Do It

Targeted Skill:

Follows directions from adults.

Materials:

I'll Say It, You Do It forms

Why

Students who do not comply with directions and requests are often difficult to deal with and problematic in school. Also, students who continually refuse to follow directions may escalate to more serious and difficult behaviors, such as tantrumming, actively defying adults, and cursing or threatening others. While there is no foolproof method for ensuring that students accept and follow directions, using a highly structured approach to giving directions and reinforcing students when they follow directions is often successful.

How

This activity is adapted from "Just Do It (Please)," found in *Practical Ideas That Really Work for Students With Disruptive, Defiant, or Difficult Behaviors* (McConnell, Ryser, & Patton, 2010a). Adults can use this strategy with individual students or adapt it for use with a large group. The long-term goal is for students to self-monitor and use self-control and eventually to recognize when they *should* follow a direction.

1. Decide on your verbal routine for giving directions. Give a direction only twice before responding and use a simple, direct format. First, give the direction, and use the word *please* (e.g., Jimmy, start your assignment, please). Next, give the direction again, beginning with the phrase "You need to . . ." (e.g., Jimmy, you need to start your assignment now).
2. As you give the direction, circle the number 1 on the I'll Say It, You Do It form. If the student follows your direction after only two statements, ask the student to cross off the number. This indicates that you gave one direction and that the student followed that one direction.
3. If the student does not follow your direction after you have given it twice, tell the student to leave the number circled, but do not cross it off. This indicates that one direction was given and the student did not follow that direction. You should also have a consequence ready to implement.
4. After 10 subsequent directions, ask the student to write the number of directions he or she followed. Set a target of 7 or 8 for direction following.
5. The student should record his or her progress on the I'll Say It, You Do It graph. This information is helpful when determining student progress, especially if the student has a behavior plan in place.

Tips

- Link positive privileges and reinforcers to the student's percentage of direction following. The higher the student's percentage, the more privileges he or she earns.
- Laminate the number form and attach it to the student's desk so the student can track his or her progress throughout the day.

Example

(1̶) (2) (3̶) (4̶) (5̶) (6) (7) (8̶) (9̶) (10)   6

Note. This idea is adapted from *Practical Ideas That Really Work for Students with Disruptive, Defiant, or Difficult Behaviors: Preschool Through Grade 4* (2nd ed., pp. 115–118), by K. McConnell, G. R. Ryser, and J. R. Patton, 2010, Austin, TX: PRO-ED. Copyright 2010 by PRO-ED, Inc. Reprinted with permission.

I'll Say It, You Do It

1   2   3   4   5   6   7   8   9   10   _____

1   2   3   4   5   6   7   8   9   10   _____

1   2   3   4   5   6   7   8   9   10   _____

1   2   3   4   5   6   7   8   9   10   _____

1   2   3   4   5   6   7   8   9   10   _____

I'll Say It, You Do It

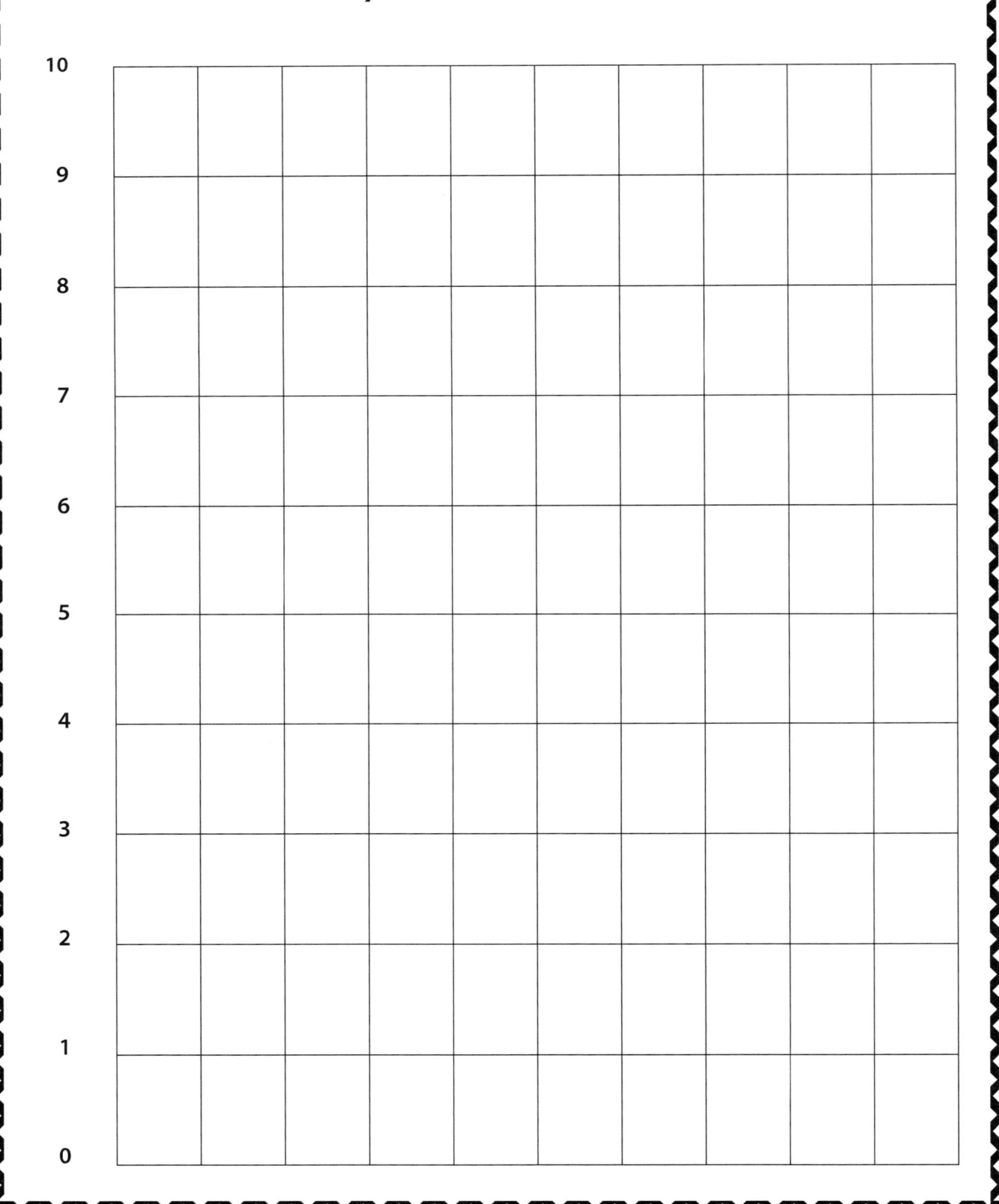

10
9
8
7
6
5
4
3
2
1
0

Skill Unit 7
Responds to nonverbal cues

Background Information

A significant amount of interpersonal communication is nonverbal (Nowicki & Duke, 1992). Because academic and social situations in schools include many opportunities to communicate nonverbally, it is important for students to perceive, interpret, and respond appropriately to nonverbal cues.

Many students with learning differences and psychosocial adjustment problems have some degree of difficulty with visual–spatial cognition, which interferes with nonverbal cue perception in social encounters (Rourke, 1995). "It is theoretically consistent that children who struggle with visual–perceptual organizational tasks would have difficulty interpreting often subtle and fleeting nonverbal social cues, such as facial expressions and various paralinguistic sources of important social information (e.g., gesture, humor)" (Petti, Volker, Shore, & Hayman-Abello, 2003, p. 24). Several studies have reported that children with nonverbal learning disabilities (NLD) or features of the NLD syndrome have difficulty with nonverbal social cue perception (e.g., facial expressions, gestures, tone of voice, context) and interpreting emotions based on those cues (Dimitrovsky, Spector, Levy-Shiff, & Vakil, 1998; Forrest, 2002; Petti et al., 2003).

Multicultural factors influence nonverbal and gestured communication as well. The amount of information that is communicated explicitly through verbal versus nonverbal means or contextual clues varies considerably from one culture to the next (Lynch & Hanson, 2004). It is important to pay attention to the culture of the child and family to understand the student's experience of responding to nonverbal cues such as eye gaze and posture.

Activities and Strategies

1. Teach the student how to recognize and respond to nonverbal communication and how to engage in small talk.
2. Help students decide which response to a social situation would most likely have a favorable outcome, and then work through the mechanics of how to carry out such a response in a competent manner.
3. Practice preventive coaching and support during the course of social interactions.
4. Help school personnel better understand the sometimes awkward or incompetent behavior of children with nonverbal learning disabilities.
5. Use group counseling to provide a safe and effective setting in which students can practice perceiving and interpreting nonverbal cues, realistic simulations, and role plays to explore and problem solve.
6. Combine teaching strategies from this unit and Skill Unit 14 to teach different interpretations of nonverbal cues based on proximity.

SKILL UNIT 7: I Read You

Targeted Skill:
Responds to nonverbal cues.

Materials:
Camera and photos taken by the student

Why

The literature suggests that students who are hostile and aggressive often misinterpret other people's facial expressions, gestures, and body language as being threatening or angry, even when they are not (Dodge & Feldman, 1990). Because of this inability to accurately read others' nonverbal language, students may then become defensive and hostile themselves. Teaching these students how to determine how others are feeling may help them choose better responses to people and prevent serious behavior problems.

How

Students who are inadequate at reading nonverbal cues can be taught how to do so. If students do not pick up the skills quickly and naturally, provide instruction. "I Read You" is a simple way to help students learn to "read" others. Here is how it works:

1. Have students learn to accurately determine other people's feelings by studying photographs of people they see daily demonstrating different facial expressions:
   - The student should talk to several adults and several students he or she sees daily and ask them if they would be willing to pose for some photographs.
   - The student should then take photographs of each person as they demonstrate various emotions and feelings (e.g., anger, sadness, frustration, confusion, impatience). The person in the photographs should include body language that models the emotions along with the facial expressions.
   - The student should keep a log that identifies each photograph, so he or she can remember which photo matches each emotion.

2. The student should work with an adult (e.g., a counselor or behavior specialist) to review the photographs and determine which feeling each picture represents. Once the photographs are labeled, the adult and the student can work together to review specific facial features and body language that provide clues about the subject's feelings. (Consider small details, such as the tilt of the person's head, the way the person is standing, the way the person's eyes look, and whether the person is smiling.)

3. After reviewing the photographs several times, the student should cover up the labels and try to identify the emotion without any cues or assistance. If the student does well,

continue the process. If the student does not do well, the adult should review the key indicators of emotion and then provide the student with more practice.

4. Eventually, the student should be able to identify how *most* people show key emotions and also how specific people he or she knows (the people in the photographs) do so.

Just in Case

Identifying how someone is feeling is not enough to ensure an appropriate response. After this step is mastered, students will then need to learn how to read and respond to a person's emotional state. This can be especially difficult if the emotions being read are intense or negative.

happy   angry   scared

SKILL UNIT 7: Emotions Drama

Targeted Skill:
Responds to nonverbal cues.

Materials:
The Boring Script handout, slips of paper with emotion words written on them

Why

Role plays provide an excellent opportunity for students to portray different emotions and see what those emotions look like when portrayed by others. Students get to see the full array of nonverbal communication that accompanies the spoken words.

How

This role-playing activity from *Self-Regulation for Kids K–12* (Tollison, Synatschk, & Logan, 2011) uses The Boring Script handout, but any script, including one written with the student, could be used. The idea is to have a script of a brief, neutral dialogue that two people can enact.

1. Write some emotion words (e.g., *angry, disappointed, happy, insulted, courteous, neutral, exasperated, sad, apologetic*) on slips of paper, and put them into a container. Give a copy of The Boring Script handout to a student, and keep one for yourself. Read through the script together once, with each of you taking a role.

2. Both performers should draw an emotion paper from the container, without showing the other person. Reread the script, but this time performers should enact each role as if he or she were experiencing the emotion that was drawn from the container.

3. Discuss the differences in the portrayal when various emotions are displayed. Have students guess both performers' emotions and give feedback about why they identified that emotion. Continue drawing emotion words and reenacting the script, or have other members of the group choose emotion words and reenact the script. Ask the students: **What indicators did you pay attention to as you decided which emotion the actors portrayed? What other words could you use to describe the emotions others showed? How did other people perceive the emotions expressed?**

© 2012 by PRO-ED, Inc.   #13936

The Boring Script

Scene: A coffee shop

Customer:	Hello, I'd like coffee with milk and a donut.
Sales clerk:	We're out of coffee.
Customer:	Oh. Out of coffee? I'll just have tea, then.
Sales clerk:	We're out of tea.
Customer:	Oh. Well, could I just have the milk, then?
Sales clerk:	Nope, no milk, either.
Customer:	What? No milk?
Sales clerk:	No milk. None at all.
Customer:	Well, I guess I will just have the frosted donut.
Sales clerk:	We're out of donuts.
Customer:	You are out of donuts?
Sales clerk:	Yup. Out.
Customer:	Well, OK, I guess I'll have to go somewhere else. Is there anywhere else I can go around here for coffee and some donuts?
Sales clerk:	Out the door and to the left. Third door down.
Customer:	Thanks. Good-bye.
Sales clerk:	Have a nice day.

Note. From *Self-Regulation for Kids K–12* (p. 207), by P. K. Tollison, K. O. Synatschk, and G. Logan, 2011, Austin, TX: PRO-ED. Copyright 2011 by PRO-ED. Used with permission.

Skill Unit 8
Demonstrates empathy for others

Background Information

Empathy is the ability to understand another's perspective and emotional state. Research also suggests that empathy is a complex phenomenon involving several component skills: a sense of self-awareness and the ability to distinguish one's own feelings from the feelings of others, taking another person's perspective, and being able to regulate one's own emotional responses. Empathy is not an attribute one either has or lacks; everyone has degrees of empathy, but even adults can have trouble with these abilities. For example, some adults would shrink from offering a wounded person first aid, not because they are callous but because they have trouble coping with their own emotional reactions to the other person's plight. For kids for whom demonstrating empathy does not come naturally, behaviors can be practiced and learned.

Activities and Strategies

- Address the students' needs, and teach them how to recover from distress. When students have secure attachment relationships, they are more likely to show sympathy and offer help to other students in distress (Kestenbaum, Farber, & Sroufe, 1989). Students are more likely to show empathic concern for others if their parents and teachers have helped them cope with negative emotions in a sympathetic, problem-solving-oriented way.
- Seize everyday opportunities to model and induce sympathetic feelings for other people. For example, if someone is being victimized (in real life, on TV, or in a book), talk to the students about how the person must feel (Pizarro & Salovey, 2002). Use moments of discomfort as opportunities to induce empathy for others.
- Praise empathic behavior. When students perform an act of kindness, tell them what they did right, and be as specific as possible. Teach students to notice when other people have behaved kindly.
- Teach nonverbal cues. Play a game of guessing what other people are feeling, and explain the specific reasons for your own guesses.
- Help students discover what they have in common with other people. Experiments suggest that students are more likely to feel empathy for individuals who are familiar or similar to them. When students discover similarities they share with other people, through humanizing the victims of distress or tragedy, they will be better able to respond with empathy.
- Simulations and role-playing experiences can give students some insight into the difficulties others have. Special blindfolds and other props can help students experience some aspects of having a disability.
- Show students how to "make a face" while they try to imagine how someone else feels. Experiments show that simply going through the motions of making a facial expression

can make us experience the associated emotion. When researchers have asked people to imitate certain facial expressions, they have detected changes in brain activity that are characteristic of the corresponding emotions. People also experience changes in heart rate, skin conductance, and body temperature (Decety & Jackson, 2004).

- To help students see themselves and others as equal, try this exercise (Wallace, 2006).
    1. Start by grounding and calming, to develop a calm but attentive mind.
    2. Ask students to focus on someone with whom they have a close relationship. Then tell them to look at themselves from that person's point of view. Ask: **Can you see the similarities between your desires and your loved one's desires? Can you see how, just like you, your friend longs to be free from pain and insecurity? This person whom you love, do you see that they are a distinct human being with both excellent qualities and defects?**
    3. Next, direct the student: **Recall someone with whom you have a conflict. Step inside this person's skin—experience their hopes, experience their fears. Stay with this practice for a while.**
    4. Realize that, like yourself, this person just wants to be happy and not experience pain. When we understand the shared quality of these experiences, we can begin to see that this person is not the true source of our own suffering. We can reach genuine acceptance of ourselves and others—with all our flaws and imperfections—and to relate to our own mind and others as works in progress.
- Help students understand the reciprocal nature of relationships and how empathy impacts our friendships. Say: **How do you feel when someone really listens and tries to understand how you feel? It's important to know that others care about us. People who take the time to really understand others are valued and appreciated as friends. Like conversations, relationships are reciprocal, which means that how each person acts influences the other person in the relationship. When we feel others care about how we feel, it often deepens our caring for others. And when we care for others, often they care even more for us. It helps us feel connected.**

SKILL UNIT 8: Showing Empathy

Targeted Skill:

Demonstrates empathy for others.

Materials:

Empathy Situations list, Empathy and Perspective Taking response form

Why

"Empathy" is the ability to understand another's perspective and emotional state while managing one's own emotional state. Showing empathy lies at the foundation of creating meaningful relationships with others. With practice, we can help students establish and improve their capacity for empathy and the ability to respond appropriately to another's situation.

How

Introduce Empathy and Perspective Taking

1. Write "Empathy" on the board, and ask the group what it means. Acknowledge and record the students' responses. Sample responses include listening to and reading someone else's verbal and nonverbal cues to make sure that you understand the person, understanding other people's points of view and feelings, saying or doing something for a person to show that you understand, and helping others.
2. Discuss the expression "putting yourself in someone else's shoes" and what it means to see a situation from different perspectives. Explain that two different people will see the same situation differently and that empathy involves being able to imagine what another person might see and feel.
3. Help the students understand the reciprocal nature of relationships and how empathy impacts our friendships.

Discuss Steps in Responding With Empathy

Say: **When you respond with empathy, you show concern and understanding for others.** Write the Empathy Steps in the board or on a poster and direct the students' attention to them.

Empathy Steps

1. Pay attention to what the other person is saying and doing.
2. Try to figure out what the person might be thinking and feeling.
3. Say or do something to show that you understand the person's perspective.
4. Ask the other person if what you did or said helped and made the person feel understood.

Discuss Each Step

1. The first step is to listen to and observe what the person is saying and how the person is acting. Look and listen to determine how the person might feel. Use the following cues to help you: facial expressions, arm and hand movements, choice of words, and tone of voice.
2. The second step is to put yourself in the other person's shoes and try to figure out what the person is thinking and feeling from his or her perspective or point of view. It might help to think about a time when you had a similar experience. If you haven't had a similar experience, then imagine what it might be like.
3. The third step is responding to the person in an empathic way. That means showing the person that you understand. You might start by saying something like "That sounds really hard . . . " "I can understand your feeling that way . . . " or "Seems like you are . . . "
4. Finally, check in with the person to see if what you said or did was helpful and if it made the person feel understood. Remember that when sharing your understanding of the other's thoughts and feelings, your interpretation may not be correct. Listen for the other person's reply to what you have said. If you were wrong, correct what you said or ask the person what else you could say or do to help.

When students' empathic response is unsuccessful, they can think about what other cues they could have looked for to better understand how the person felt.

Role-Play Empathic Responses

1. Distribute the Empathy Situations list and have pairs of students take turns role-playing, with one reading the situation aloud and the other giving an empathic response.
2. After each role play, discuss and evaluate how the role play went and how the empathy giver did well in their response. Ask students if something similar has ever happened to them, or if they could imagine how such a situation would feel.

Note. Adapted from *Resilience Builder Program for Children and Adolescents* (pp. 184–186), by M. K. Alvord, B. Zucker, and J. J. Grados, 2011, Champaign, IL: Research Press. Adapted with permission.

Empathy Situations

Your friend has just found out that he was not picked to be in the school play, something your friend wanted very much.	Your friend is angry because the teacher thinks she cheated on a test, when actually she did not.
Your friend made poor behavior choices when angry at a sports practice, and the coach has informed your friend that she cannot play for the next three games.	A boy in your class is upset because he was teased in the cafeteria.
Your friend's parent has just told him that they are moving to another state.	Your friend has just told you that her parents are getting divorced.

Note. Adapted from *Resilience Builder Program for Children and Adolescents* (p. 189), by M. K. Alvord, B. Zucker, and J. J. Grados, 2011, Champaign, IL: Research Press. Adapted with permission.

Name _____ Date _____

Empathy and Perspective Taking

Observe someone at home or at school who is expressing strong emotions. Think about how he or she might be feeling and how you might respond to show that you understand. Record the following information:

1. Whom did you observe?
2. What was the situation?
3. What facial expression did the person have?
4. How did the person move his or her body?
5. What words did the person use?
6. What tone of voice did the person use?
7. What do you think the person was thinking?
8. How do you think the person felt?
9. What do you think someone could do or say to this person that may make him or her feel understood or feel better?
10. How would you know the person felt understood?

Note. Adapted from *Resilience Builder Program for Children and Adolescents* (p. 190), by M. K. Alvord, B. Zucker, and J. J. Grados, 2011, Champaign, IL: Research Press. Adapted with permission.

© 2012 by PRO-ED, Inc.   #13936

Skill Unit 9
Works productively in a group

Background Information

Research suggests that students who have problems with aggression, especially bullying behaviors, have problems with relationships, including those with peers and family members (Pepler, Jiang, Craig, & Connolly, 2008). Supporting students as they build relationships with others is a proactive approach to preventing conflicts. Adults can play an important role in helping students who are unsuccessful at relationships improve their social skills and gain a sense of belonging in the school community. This is especially important with students who do not participate in clubs, sports teams, or school interest groups.

Activities and Strategies

A simple strategy for helping students connect with others is to establish student-partner and small-group activities. These activities should be designed and implemented by adults.

- Decide the size of the group—usually from two to six students, depending on the nature of the task and the time available.
- Assign students to groups, preferably by heterogeneous grouping rather than by student ability or students self-selection. Maintain the group assignments through each new task. Allow time for each group member to get to know each other through the work of several tasks. Consider changing groupings once a month.
- Arrange the room so that groups can work together without disrupting other groups.
- Plan instructional materials to promote interdependence. Give only one copy of the materials to the group.
- Assign roles to promote interdependence. Use titles such as "summarizer," "researcher," "recorder," "encourager," and "observer."
- Structure individual accountability and group assessment so that the individual's rewards are based both on his or her scores and on the average for the groups as a whole.
- Model, explain, and elicit examples of appropriate behaviors, including students taking turns, using personal names, and listening carefully to one another, and encourage everyone to participate.
- Teach students how to brainstorm:
  1. Ask for ideas
  2. Accept without judgment
  3. Go around until everyone is out of ideas
- Monitor student behavior. Circulate around the room to listen to and observe groups in action. Note problems in completing assignments and working cooperatively.
- Allow opportunities for groups to orally report their findings to the whole class.

- Ask for and give feedback from each group about how well the members worked together and accomplished tasks, and how they could improve.
- Do not intervene with the students' ability to accomplish a task. Allow students to identify a path of inquiry and negotiate the path in collaboration with others.

Here are some additional, specific structures that school personnel can establish to help students build positive relationships and gain a sense of belonging at school.

Peer Partners for Assignments

When a disruptive or acting-out student is in the classroom, assign peer partners carefully. Consider making short- rather than long-term assignments, and choose a partner for the challenging student who is unafraid and unlikely to be a victim if the acting-out student is a bully. A positive role model with a strong character and confidence is the ideal partner.

Lunch-Bunch Participants

Adults at school can meet with individual students or small groups at lunch time, which will allow them to get to know students better than is possible in large groups. Adults should consider meeting with the difficult or challenging student alone several times before inviting other students to join them, and then give careful consideration to the make-up of the whole group. Getting to know the student and building trust is critical if the acting-out student is to begin building healthy, positive relationships at school.

Leadership or Service Teams

Many students benefit from and enjoy service and leadership activities. For students who are not accustomed to contributing to their schools or communities, start with small projects that have immediate results, for example, working outside in a school garden, helping with campus-wide recycling, collecting clothing or school supplies for younger students, helping select and arrange music for assemblies, and making morning announcements.

Cross-Age Tutoring

Students who have difficulty interacting successfully with their same-age peers may be more sensitive and caring with younger children. Adults can design specific cross-age tutoring activities such as reading aloud to younger students, tutoring a young student who is struggling academically, or playing games with a small group of young children. Of course, adequate adult supervision should be maintained at all times.

Community-Based Volunteering

Setting up connections with community service groups to deliver meals, visit nursing-home residents, work in community gardens, or help with home building are all useful and rewarding activities that older students may enjoy and that may give them a connection to their community and their neighbors.

Follow-Up

An adult (e.g., counselor, teacher, administrator) should follow up with the student after any of these relationship-building activities. During the follow-up, the adult should encourage the student to self-evaluate his or her performance when interacting with others and also reflect on how the experience made him or her feel. It is critical that students who have been aggressive toward others develop an understanding of others' feelings as well as empathy and caring for them. Without such progress toward socialization, these students may not develop the self-regulation needed to maintain a positive approach to school, their families, and people in their community.

SKILL UNIT 9: Get Together

Targeted Skill:

Works productively in a group.

Materials:

Getting Together: Here's What Worked! self-reflection form

Why

Teaching students with diverse abilities and different learning rates can effectively be achieved through cooperative learning. In addition to developing social skills and facilitating classroom management, working in teams or groups reflects the way much of the work world is conducted. The work world is often a collaborative, cooperative enterprise, but the ability to work in a group does not always come naturally to every student. Teachers can facilitate good teamwork skills.

How

Involve all members of a group in a hands-on learning activity by assigning and teaching roles such as facilitator, scribe, materials manager, and timekeeper. Rotate or reassign the roles so that every student can be involved in every part of the process and have a chance to play his or her favorite role.

Getting Together: Here's What Worked! is a self-reflection tool that students can use as they work on their group skills. For younger students, simplify the language and discuss it verbally. Older students can complete the form and discuss it with an adult.

Getting Together: Here's What Worked!

Name: _____ Day or week: _____

Adult monitor: _____ Class: _____

1. What I did that required me to work with another person:
   _____

2. My responsibilities included:
   _____

3. I got along with the other person:

   Not at all   Okay   Great

   1   2   3   4   5

4. I learned:
   _____

5. To get along better with others I can:
   _____

6. I enjoyed this experience:

   Not at all   Okay   Great

   1   2   3   4   5

7. Next time I work with a partner or small group, one thing I can improve is:
   _____

© 2012 by PRO-ED, Inc. #13936

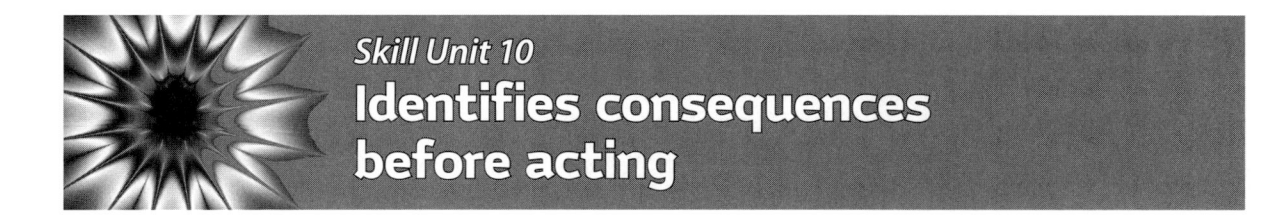

Skill Unit 10
Identifies consequences before acting

Background Information

Predicting the consequences of an action requires complicated, sometimes rapid, biological and behavioral responses. For students, age is a factor in their ability to predict or identify consequences and then make good decisions based on those consequences. Very young children often do not have a long-term perspective or enough experience to predict what will happen in their future.

In addition to age, disabilities, such as attention-deficit/hyperactivity disorder or autism may result in inattention, impulsivity, and hyperactivity, which also affect decision making. Research indicates that specific brain functions are related to the detection of stimuli or events in the environment and that other brain functions determine a person's self-monitoring after environmental factors are recognized. The two functions do not have to be related or in sync (Blakemore, Rees, & Frith, 1998). The brain is organized to function as an integrated whole, with different brain centers communicating through neural connections. Healthy neural integration enables contextualization and the integration of memory and experience into language. It also allows the ability to access and assess details of the situation and use past experiences to make decisions about how best to respond. Neural integration enables whole brain processing and emotion to be modulated by a "wedge of cognition"; that is, it creates the opportunity for reflection and adaptive response to guide action (Saxe et al., 2007). Healthy neural integration includes the following:

- Regulating the body's physical reactions
- Regulating emotion
- Having emotionally attuned interpersonal communication
- Creating a sense about other's subjective experience
- Having response flexibility, taking in information, thinking, considering options, and producing an adaptive response
- Creating self-awareness and autobiographical memory
- Morality (Siegel, 2003)

Not only our brain but also our ethical and moral framework come into play when we recognize the consequences of our actions. There are many perspectives on consequences in philosophical and ethical literature, most of which relate to principles of right and wrong. Because our understanding and commitment to ethical and moral beliefs affect how we live our lives, they are important to address with students. Using cognitive–behavioral strategies that ask students to identify consequences, think through their actions, rehearse what they will do, and practice repeatedly is an effective approach to decision making. Counting to 10, taking deep breaths, or considering options are valuable reregulating tools that can be very effective with frustrated or irritated students (Levine & Kline, 2007). The same tools will not be effective with dysregulated students, however. When students have impaired neural integration, their brains are dominated by automatic responses that do not access and use knowledge from one context or experience to another. Students who can recognize emotional shifts by tuning in to their own early somatic signals of becoming dysregulated allow a wedge of cognition that will help them calm down and access information that will allow them to make more adaptive responses. Dysregulation is a neurological problem that has behavioral consequences, and effective interventions take this into account.

This section contains activities that are related to the first step in the cognitive–behavioral process—identifying consequences. They can help students learn to identify and consider consequences and comprehensive strategies that will support them in mastering this skill.

Activities and Strategies

- Remember that identifying consequences is just one step in the overall process of making good decisions. Once students have mastered this skill, they may still need help with decision making.
- Practice, practice, practice. Some students have never considered the consequences of their actions, and it will take some time and a lot of practice for them to learn how to do this.
- Consistently emphasize the impact that an individual's actions have on others. Stress empathy.
- Remind students that they have choices. Just because they have made bad decisions in the past doesn't mean that the pattern has to continue in the future. People can change their behavior.
- Remind students that they have choices and that the choices they make will determine the consequences they face. Present options throughout the day by telling them, "You have a choice. You can _____, or you can _____. Think about the consequences of each choice."

Class Discussions

Help students identify likely consequences to their actions:

- Begin the day or class period with a short discussion of things that are likely to happen in class or in school. The discussion can be quick and simple or specific and thorough, depending on the age of your students. Here are some possible topics:
  1. Problems that might happen; how we can handle them
  2. Changes that might occur; what to do differently
  3. Possible unexpected events (things that do not happen often but that could occur); what to do about them
- Discuss why people do some things and not others. Again, the level of discussion will depend on students' ages and levels of maturity. Here are some issues to discuss:
  1. Why some things are "right" and some things are "wrong"
  2. Whether some actions are always wrong or always right, or whether it depends on circumstances

3. How our actions can help or hurt other people
4. How we know what will happen after we do something (past experience, observation, or an informed guess)

- Explore the students' understanding of actions that will affect only individuals and actions that affect groups of people or the whole society. Use everyday, real-life examples that are relevant to students. Here are some topics and questions that would lend themselves to this kind of discussion:
    1. What difference does it make if you cheat or steal? If no one catches you, does it really hurt anything?
    2. If you are rude to people or mean to others, what will they think of you? Will they treat you differently in the future?
    3. If other students are doing something wrong, like bullying another student or stealing in the cafeteria, would you join in? Why or why not?

SKILL UNIT 10: If/Then

Targeted Skill:
Identifies consequences before acting.

Materials:
If/Then form

Why

To help students make decisions, make sure they first know the consequences of their actions. Both adults and children make rash decisions and refuse to consider the consequences thoughtfully or thoroughly. The "If/Then" strategy should help students clearly identify possible consequences of their actions, be honest and recognize what might happen, and see that some consequences are predictable.

How

Plan ahead with students who are impulsive or easily dysregulated or who typically do not consider the consequences of their actions. Have a short, small group or one-to-one meeting and ask students to suggest things that often happen to them and how they might handle those things. Show them the "If/Then" format. First, think of some typical situations that occur and that may cause problems. Next, in the "If" column, write down what you could do in response to the situation. Finally, in the "Then" side, write down the consequences of your actions. Here are some examples:

- You don't understand something the teacher explains in class. You want to rip up your paper and leave the classroom. *If* you do, *then* you will get sent to the office and get in trouble. However, *if* you raise your hand and ask for help, *then* the teacher or another student can help you and you can finish your work without getting in trouble.
- *If* someone teases you and you hit that person, *then* you will probably get sent to the office and have to go to in-school the suspension or detention. On the other hand, *if* you ignore the teasing and just walk away or report it to a teacher, *then* you will not get in trouble and your day will go smoothly.
- *If* you see someone's lunch money in a desk and you know no one is looking and you take it, *then* you may feel guilty, have to worry about getting caught, or know that people may not trust you. You may also get caught eventually and have to pay back the money and know that everyone thinks you are a thief and doesn't like you. But *if* you leave the money and people know you didn't take it, *then* they will probably trust you more.

© 2012 by PRO-ED, Inc.   #13936

Just in Case

Teachers or counselors using the "If/Then" strategy might have to repeat it several times. Students may be reluctant to suggest situations at first, but once you have built up trust with them, they should offer scenarios themselves. Focus on the "Then" part of the form, and help students be realistic and honest about what the consequences for their actions will be. Include both positive and negative consequences so that students see that the choices they make are important.

Name _____   Date _____

If/Then

Complete the If/Then form by adding actions to the "If" side and probable consequences to the "Then" side for each situation. Repeat the situation and choose two different actions.

In this situation . . .	If you . . .	Then . . .

© 2012 by PRO-ED, Inc.   #13936

SKILL UNIT 10: Best Guess

Targeted Skill:

Identifies consequences before acting.

Materials:

Best Guess cards

Why

Using everyday situations as teaching opportunities is an effective way to give students a chance to practice identifying consequences that they might not otherwise consider. "Best Guess" gives students opportunities to tell you what will happen in different situations.

How

Tape Best Guess reminder cards to students' desks, or post larger versions of them in the classroom. When you see a situation in which a student needs to make a choice about what to do or how to respond, refer to the Best Guess card. Ask the student to look at the question, "What do you think will happen?" Repeat the question, and ask the student for an honest answer. The student can make a choice about what to do and what not to do once he or she realizes what the consequences of the actions will be.

What do you think will happen?

BEST GUESS

_____

What do you think will happen?

BEST GUESS

_____

What do you think will happen?

BEST GUESS

_____

SKILL UNIT 10: Door Number 1 or Door Number 2

Targeted Skill:
Identifies consequences before acting.

Materials:
None

Why

Help students understand the consequences for their actions by teaching them to visualize. Learning to visualize gives students an opportunity to practice identifying consequences and making decisions.

How

Ask students to close their eyes and think about two different actions they could take in response to a situation. Here is an example.

- What are two things you could do if someone accuses you of something you didn't do? Think of two different choices you could make. For example, you could hit him and call him a liar, or you could explain that he is wrong and move away.
- Now, picture yourself opening a door. When you open the door, you see your teacher, friends, or family. If you choose the first action, what will it look and sound like? How will you feel? What will the people you know think of you? What will happen to you afterwards?
- Now, picture yourself opening the second door. When you open this door, you again see your teacher, friends, or family. But you choose the second option. What will your action look and sound like? How will you feel this time? What will people think of you, and how will they react? What do you think will happen in this picture?

Explain any visualization strategy process to the student, and then give him or her a chance to practice. Practice visualizing in private at first, so the student does not feel self-conscious or embarrassed.

SKILL UNIT 10: If You Do, If You Don't

Targeted Skill:
Identifies consequences before acting.

Materials:
None

Why

"If You Do, If You Don't" is a comprehensive strategy that can be used to help students identify consequences for their actions. This strategy is part of an overall classroom management system. It is taken from *Practical Ideas That Really Work for Students With Disruptive, Defiant, or Difficult Behaviors, Second Edition* (McConnell et al., 2010a, 2010b).

"If You Do, If You Don't" is a method of establishing and teaching both positive and reductive consequences in the classroom. The idea is to develop, communicate, teach, and practice these consequences, and then implement them consistently. When teachers implement consequences consistently, students learn them more quickly and know exactly what the consequences will be.

How

Create a two-column list of consequences: What will occur if students *do* follow the rules in the first column and what will occur if they *do not* follow the rules in the second column. Arrange the list from least to most serious. Post a large version in the classroom and review the rules and consequences with students regularly.

Just in Case

Focus on the positive consequences.

Explain that extremely disruptive or dangerous behaviors require an immediate and serious response that will not follow the continuum.

Note. This idea is adapted from *Practical Ideas That Really Work for Students with Disruptive, Defiant, or Difficult Behaviors: Preschool Through Grade 4* (2nd ed., pp. 61–62), by K. McConnell, G. R. Ryser, and J. R. Patton, 2010, Austin, TX: PRO-ED. Copyright 2010 by PRO-ED, Inc. Reprinted with permission.

Skill Unit 11
Manages transitions

Background Information

Transitional activities decrease the time students engage in academic activities and provide opportunities for students with behavior difficulties to have serious problems. Transition time has been estimated to be more than 70 minutes per day. Using effective transitions in the classroom helps teachers to minimize disruptions and behavior problems, maximize instructional time, and maintain optimal learning conditions (Cangelosi, 2000; Smith, Polloway, Patton, & Dowdy, 2001). When students are able to manage transitions, they can move from one activity to the next efficiently and begin the next task in both formal and informal settings.

Activities and Strategies

- Ensure that students understand and follow transition cues.
- For noninstructional transitions, such as moving from the classroom to the library, clearly explain the procedures and model, practice, and reinforced them until students can carry them out quickly and appropriately. Establish time limits for completing transitions, and then reinforce adherence to the limits. For example, record the amount of time it takes for students to get ready for a lesson. Then, challenge the students to reduce this amount of time to a targeted goal. Establish a cue, either verbal or nonverbal, that all students will recognize as a signal to make a transition to a new activity.
- Circulate among students during transition times, and attend to individual student's needs and questions, help them prepare for the next task, and calm any disruptions before they escalate (Burden, 2003).
- Prominently post and adhere to a daily or weekly schedule, and make certain students know of any changes ahead of time (Olson & Platt, 2000).
- Minimize the number of transitions during the day. In some instances, teachers may assign a peer to accompany the student from class to class.
- Prepare difficult students for changes by mentioning the amount of time remaining in a work period and by taking the student aside to explain any change in routine that might occur later in the day. Time countdowns and advance warnings help the student with difficulties anticipate changes and respond more appropriately.
- Help students regulate their emotions and behavior prior to initiating a transition.
- Reinforce positive transition behavior, and facilitate the student's awareness of how he or she made it work.

SKILL UNIT 11: Plan Ahead to Keep Your Head

Targeted Skill:

Manages transitions.

Materials:

Plan Ahead to Keep Your Head plan

Why

Social researchers have long recognized that individuals often behave differently in groups than they do alone. In schools, disruptive and even dangerous behavior can be contagious. Situations can start as mild problems and escalate to serious problems very quickly. For students who have poor self-management skills, staying calm when others are out of control can be a real challenge. It is important that adults teach students some effective strategies for remaining calm when other students are not. Remaining calm will not only keep students from getting in trouble, it may help prevent serious problems with the whole group.

How

There are several strategies that students can use to maintain their composure when other students are acting out, disrupting instruction, or challenging adults in school. "Plan Ahead to Keep Your Head" can be used as one component of a more comprehensive strategy. These steps can help adults teach students to plan ahead and keep their heads:

1. Identify problematic or volatile situations.
   - Adults may want to help *all* students identify situations in school that are likely to escalate into serious disruption or have the potential to become harmful. Identifying the problem situations early is the key. Adults should discuss with students things to look out for, including students who exhibit the following:
     - Yelling or talking loudly
     - Demonstrating aggressive body language, such as clenched fists, standing too close, or "getting in another's face"
     - Congregating in a large group
     - Cursing
     - Taunting or threatening someone
     - Throwing or destroying materials
     - Running in areas of the school where it's not allowed
     - Pushing and shoving each other
     - Threatening adults or other students
     - Others: _____
     - Others: _____
   - Teams of teachers, administrators, counselors, psychologists, or behavior specialists can talk to all students about

these potentially volatile situations with the understanding that not all will become explosive but all should be watched carefully.

2. Help each student develop a plan for what to do in a volatile situation.
   - Here are some options students can consider and include on their "Plan Ahead and Keep Your Head" plans. The student and adult should plan these options together so that both agree on acceptable responses, understood signals, and clear expectations for actions such as leaving a classroom.
     - In class, I will put my head down, do some work, and ignore the situation.
     - I will just walk away if I am in a common area of the school.
     - I will move to a counselor's or administrator's office.
     - I will quietly go to the bathroom (after signaling an adult who knows the plan).
     - I will move to a quiet area in the classroom if I am in class.
     - I will make sure that I don't talk at all.
     - I will keep my hands on my materials or in my pockets.
     - If I need to go somewhere, I will find a route that avoids problems.
     - Others: _____
     - Others: _____

3. Encourage and reward the student when he or she follows the plan.
   - Provide encouragement and reinforcement to the challenging student who not only develops a good plan for volatile situations but actually uses it in problematic situations. Discuss available choices with the student, provide feedback, and then follow through consistently when the student does well. There is space at the bottom of the plan that adults can use as a contract with the student.

Just in Case

There is no one right way for students to behave when a problem situation arises. They should identify several alternatives so that they can choose some they are comfortable using and that have some flexibility. What works in the classroom may not work in the school office. This type of intervention can be used with young children as well as older students, but coaching and support from adults will likely be critical for student success.

Name _____ Date _____

Plan Ahead and Keep Your Head
My Plan

When I see or hear these:

I will do one of these:

Afterwords, I will check in with _____. If I do well, I will earn _____, and the principal and my parents or guardian will receive a positive note about my choices.

© 2012 by PRO-ED, Inc.   #13936

Name _____ Date _____

Plan Ahead and Keep Your Head
My Plan

When I see or hear these:

| Yelling and cursing | Someone getting mad | Shoving and pushing | | |

I will do one of these:

| Keep quiet | Stay calm | Walk away | | |

Afterwords, I will check in with _____ **. If I do well, I will earn** _____, **and the principal and my parents or guardian will receive a positive note about my choices.**

© 2012 by PRO-ED, Inc.   #13936

SKILL UNIT 11: Morning Meeting

Targeted Skill:
Manages transitions.

Materials:
Visual Schedules, Change Cards, Social Skills Narrative

Why

Schools are busy places, and changes occur all the time. Changes, transitions, and new situations in school, even minor ones, can have a big impact on students, especially students with disabilities such as an autism spectrum disorder or attention-deficit/hyperactivity disorder. Transitions and changes can cause anxiety, stress, feelings of loss of control, and vulnerability. Many students may overreact or underreact to specific triggers when these feelings occur.

Educators have gained an understanding of how important it is to help students deal with transitions and new situations. Strategies such as visual signals, cues and warnings, change plans, and social problem-solving stories have all been introduced into students' programs and even into the curricula for some schools. Teachers can use the "Morning Meeting" activity to systematically teach students how to recognize and cope with new situations, transitions, and other changes without becoming agitated or overreacting. Along with learning strategies for dealing with changes, students will need reminding, reviewing, coaching, and even reteaching. A morning meeting with the student is the perfect opportunity for adults to use these approaches.

How

An adult who has the time and commitment (e.g., teacher, counselor, instructional assistant, administrator) must agree to lead the morning meeting, in which the adult and student work together on simple steps that will help prevent transition-related problems. Here are some key points that will help make the morning meetings more productive:

1. Schedule and meet at the same time and in the same place each morning.
2. Keep the meeting short but productive so that the student does not miss valuable class time.
3. Have some easy-to-use tools available, and use them consistently.
4. When the student is doing well, meet every other day instead of every day (however, do not discontinue the meetings too soon, or the student may not be as successful).
5. Throughout the day, if time permits, check in with the student to see how things are going. Coach if necessary.
6. After a change, transition, or other new situation, process the student's success. Problem solve if things didn't go right, and create a new plan if necessary.

7. When changes and transitions occur and the student does well, congratulate and reinforce that student's success.

Here are preventive strategies to discuss with the student in the morning meeting:

- For younger children, use a visual schedule for each school day. Every picture will represent a class, person, or activity. If there is a change, such as a substitute teacher for the day, the picture of the regular teacher should be removed and a "substitute" card put in its place. Here is a visual example.

- You can also use Change Cards. These cards warn a student of a change and provide encouragement for the transition.

- Write a social-skills narrative that provides suggestions about how to handle new situations. The adult will need to help the student write the story and also rehearse or practice it with the student as needed.

Daily Schedule

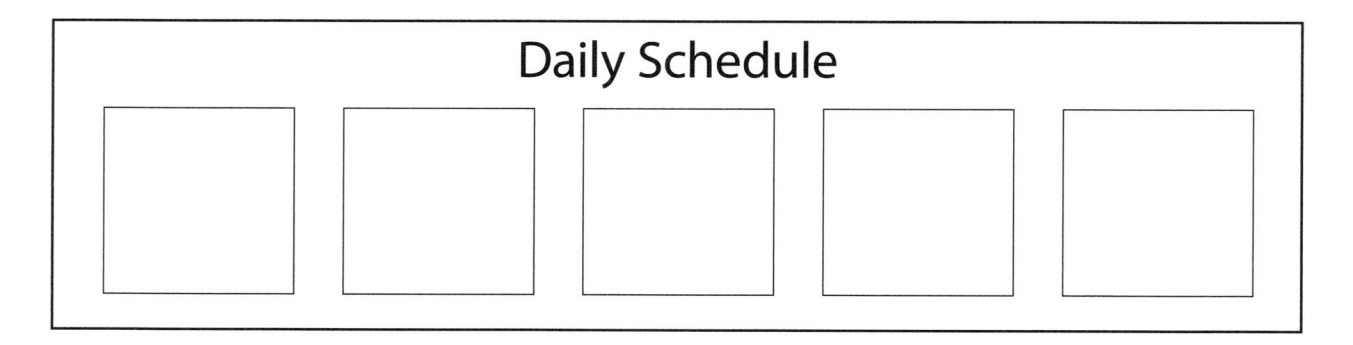

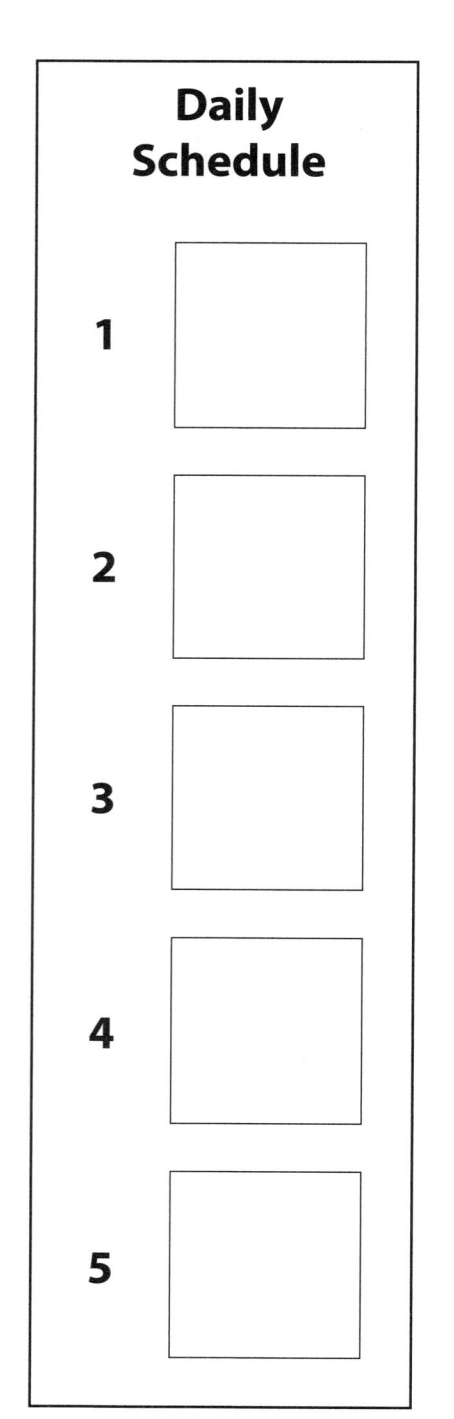

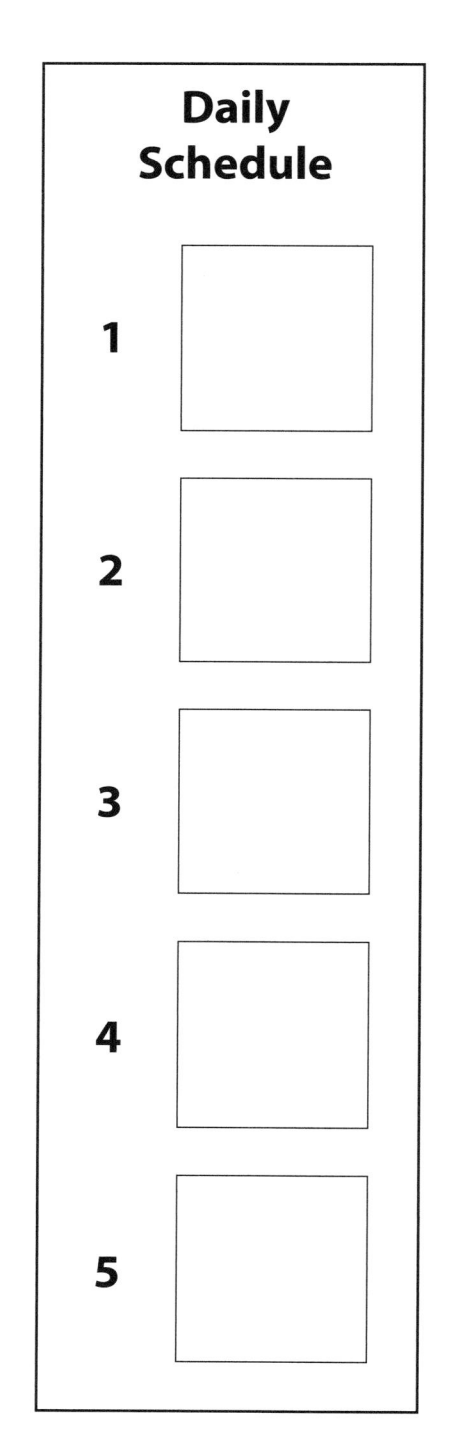

Daily Schedule

1
2
3
4
5

Daily Schedule

1
2
3
4
5

© 2012 by PRO-ED, Inc. #13936

Stay Cool

Stay Cool

Change is okay!

Change is okay!

Change is okay!

© 2012 by PRO-ED, Inc.   #13936

Skill Unit 12
Uses resources for obtaining help when getting upset

Background Information

Why do some students ask for help when others don't? Weimer's (2009) research related to students' willingness to ask for help with academic assignments indicated that the following factors are linked to seeking assistance:

- Knowledge of available assistance
- Positive experience with asking for help
- Cultural identity, especially if students feel "different"
- Gender (women are often more likely to ask for help than men)
- Belief that the student is "bothering" someone

For students who become angry, agitated, or aggressive, asking for help can be particularly difficult. They may not think or react logically and clearly and may feel embarrassed or foolish if they ask for help in front of their peers.

Activities and Strategies

- Model asking for assistance in a calm way. Teach students what to do and say.
- Provide an environment that is safe and predictable. Ask students to role-play these skills, either with a small group or with individual students.
- Be aware of the nonverbal signs students demonstrate when they are getting agitated. This will allow you to predict when students are about to lose control and cue them to ask for help before they do.
- Make sure you are responsive when students ask for help, so they are likely to do so again.
- Make sure the student knows the steps needed to calm down, so that after asking for help, he or she is able to accept it.
- Continue to focus on your positive relationships with students. When students trust adults, they are more likely to ask them for help.

SKILL UNIT 12: Need Help? Just Ask for It

Targeted Skill:
Uses resources for obtaining help when getting upset.

Materials:
Need Help? Just Ask for It cards; gestures that mean, I Need Help; Because You Asked . . . tickets

Procedure

Sometimes students are too upset to stop and ask someone to help them. In some cases, they do not know how to ask for help or feel uncomfortable doing so. This two-part activity includes (a) adult prompting, so that when adults see a student about to lose control, they prompt and encourage the student; and (b) student requesting, which involves a student asking for help if he or she is frustrated, upset, or about to lose control. Here's how this simple strategy works:

1. First, recognize when a student is beginning to get angry, upset, frustrated, or agitated. Common signs include these:
   - The student's body tenses up. The adult may notice clenched fists or tight shoulders.
   - The student may look down or look away, or stare at someone.
   - The student may seem agitated (e.g., moving around, tapping a pencil, humming, getting out of his or her seat, talking out loud, throwing papers or pencil, ripping up things).
   - The student may get red in the face or begin to cry.
   - The student may have sudden movements (e.g., standing up, leaving a group, slamming down books or notebooks).
   - The student may start to mumble or whine.
   - Others: _____

2. When these behaviors are observed, use signals or prompts that will encourage the student to ask for help before he or she has a tantrum, meltdown, or physical explosion. These prompts and cues can include the following:
   - A Need Help? Just Ask for It card
   - A color system signal (e.g., a red sign on the corner of the desk means, "I need some help.")
   - A physical gesture that only the adult and student recognize
   - Calmly and quietly moving to the student's desk and privately asking if he or she needs assistance

3. Once the adult recognizes the student's need for assistance and provides the opportunity for the student to ask, the student should use a simple, calm request. Teach and practice this simple request ahead of time.

4. After the student successfully requests help, the adult should provide it quickly and calmly. The student should then receive verbal and possibly tangible praise for asking for help instead of blowing up or losing control.

Student Cards

| I need help. | Can you help me, please? |

Teacher Cards

| Need help? | I can tell you need help. |

Student ASL Signs

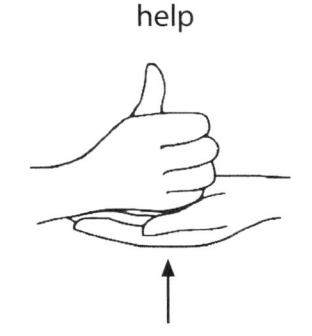

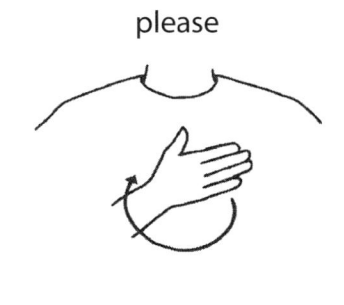

help

please

© 2012 by PRO-ED, Inc.   #13936

You asked for help, so you can ask for:

- ☐ Time to play a game
- ☐ An extra trip to the library
- ☐ An extra line leader day
- ☐ A day to sit wherever you like
- ☐ A phone call to someone special
- ☐ _____

You asked for help, so you can ask for:

1

2

3

© 2012 by PRO-ED, Inc. #13936

SKILL UNIT 12: After and Before

Targeted Skill:

Uses resources for obtaining help when getting upset.

Materials:

After and Before forms

Why

Agitated, upset, or out-of-control students are likely not thinking clearly or processing information effectively. When a student is in the middle of an outburst or crisis, adults should focus their efforts on deescalation. Only after the student has calmed down can thoughtful problem solving occur. Ideally, the problem-solving process will include not only reflection on what happened and what went wrong but also on what the student can do differently next time. There are many options for debriefing after a crisis. "After and Before" should help keep the process simple and to the point.

How

This strategy includes a process for debriefing with a student after he or she has had an outburst or crisis and provides a format for planning ahead so that the student does not repeat the disruptive or dangerous behavior. This strategy can be implemented after the crisis has been completely deescalated. Before beginning, the student should clean up any materials or furniture that he or she disrupted during the crisis. The student should also move alone to a calm, quiet work area. After ensuring the safety of people and property, implement the "After and Before" strategy using the following steps:

1. Make sure that the student is demonstrating calm, productive behavior.
   - After a crisis, assign the student work that can be done independently. Indicators that the student is calming down and is ready to be debriefed include the student maintaining attention to the assignment, working steadily to complete the assignment, and completing the assignment in a reasonable period of time.
2. After the student has completed the assignment, discuss the incident with the student and ask him or her to complete the "After and Before" form.
   - When completing this form, discuss each question and response with the student. If the student is reluctant to respond, ask the student to write his or her responses first, and then have the discussion. A version for younger students allows them to draw or place pictures or icons on the problem-solving form. For both younger and older students, having an honest and productive discussion with the adult is the key.

- Avoid reminding the student of what he or she did wrong (*after* the incident). While it is important for the student to take responsibility, the idea is to plan ahead so that *before* the next incident can occur, the student has a plan for reacting and responding differently.

Just in Case

This strategy does not take the place of crisis intervention actions that are needed to deescalate a crisis or other volatile situation. It should only be used *after* everyone is safe and the student is calm. Moving on *without* problem solving and processing often results in the student repeating the behavior, without any positive changes.

Name _____ Date _____

After and Before

1. What did you do? Describe your behavior.
   _____
   _____

2. What happened right before you behaved this way?
   _____
   _____

3. What did you want? (e.g., Attention/control/get out of class/avoid the assignment/get back at the adult/get revenge for something/to get sent home/don't know)
   _____

4. Did you get what you wanted?   YES   NO

5. What can you do differently next time this situation occurs?
   _____
   _____

6. What help will you need?
   _____
   _____

7. Who would you like to help you?
   _____

8. How can you ask for this help?
   _____

9. Do you think you can be successful at this new behavior?   YES   NO

Student Signature: _____
Adult Signature: _____

© 2012 by PRO-ED, Inc.   #13936

Name _____ Date _____

After and Before

1. What did you do?
   Draw or place a picture of your behavior.

2. Why did you do this?
   Draw or place a picture of what happened or how you were feeling.

3. What did you want to happen?
   Draw or place a picture of what you wanted.

4. What will you do differently next time?
   Draw yourself doing something different.

5. Who can help you?
   Draw a picture of someone you can ask for help.

6. Can you do it?   ☺   ☹

Sign your name here. _____

The adult will sign here. _____

© 2012 by PRO-ED, Inc.   #13936

Skill Unit 13
Attends to task, ignores distractions

Background Information

A strong predictor of academic achievement is the amount of time students actively engage in learning (Gettinger & Ball, 2011). This link between time and learning is one of the most enduring and consistent findings in educational research. On-task time, or engaged time, is the proportion of instructional time during which students are cognitively and behaviorally on task or engaged in learning, as evidenced by paying attention, completing work, interacting with peers, taking notes, listening, solving problems, or engaging in relevant discussion. Three major factors promote high rates of academic engaged time: (a) classroom management, (b) effective instruction, and (c) student-mediated strategies. Students themselves determine the extent to which they spend academic engaged time in school. Although many best practices for increasing academic engaged time emphasize managerial and instructional strategies external to the learner, students can also take an active role in maximizing their own learning time. Student-mediated best practices emphasize cognitive and affective learner characteristics and involve individual students in the regulation of their own engagement. Maximizing cognitive engagement among students requires explicit training in cognitive learning strategies, self-monitoring skills, and self-management behaviors (Zimmerman, Greenberg, & Weinstein, 1994).

Activities and Strategies

- For students with serious attention difficulties, design interventions that are based on assessment data gathered before and after interventions are implemented and tailor them to meet the unique needs of the student. Examine data regarding possible environmental functions of inattentive behavior. Use a functional assessment to determine what might be reinforcing the behavior and what could be done proactively to encourage the desired behavior.
- With the student, consider times in the past when he or she had been somewhat successful at staying on task and ignoring distractions, even in a different setting. Ask, "What could you use from that experience to plan how to achieve your goal of staying on task in this class?" What would be the first small sign that you are staying on task more?"
- Teaching students how to use cognitive strategies can increase their academic engaged time because they learn to approach learning tasks in a structured, organized, and efficient manner. For example, the use of story mapping or question generation strategies during individual reading periods enhance learning and the retention of material because students are cognitively engaged and interacting with the text.
- Review with students some of the somatic awareness and mindful awareness practices learned in previous units. Practice maintaining focus during an exercise, while letting

distracting thoughts go by. Help students notice sensations in their bodies before their attention from the task begins to stray. Help them identify statements they can make to themselves about refocusing.

- When organizational skills are a concern, work with students on a checklist of preparatory behaviors for getting ready to work, which might include having materials, attending to instructions, and being free of distractions. Remind students about expected behaviors before the start of the activity.
- Circulate throughout the classroom to monitor student behavior and provide feedback in an unobtrusive fashion.
- Use nonverbal cues and signals to redirect a student while teaching others.
- Use self-correcting techniques to teach students to monitor their own learning. Flash cards, answer tapes, overlays, and checking stations are just a few instructional tools that are effective for increasing self-checking behaviors in the classroom.
- Teach students to observe and record the occurrence of their own behaviors. For instance, students might be taught to recognize and record instances of on-task behavior during academic work. Typically, an auditory or visual signal (e.g., beep from a timer, hand signal from the teacher) is used periodically to signal students to observe their current behavior. Kern, Dunlap, Childs, and Clarke (1994) increased engagement time by having students note whether they were or were not on task at signaled intervals. This type of self-monitoring can be used alone or, more typically, in combination with other self-management procedures. Lam, Cole, Shapiro, and Bambara (1994) indicated that it may be more effective to have students monitor task completion or accuracy rather than simply monitoring attentive behavior.
- Use simple cues, such as touching a child on the shoulder. Self-recording has been found to significantly increase students' engagement in academic tasks.
- Set up a self-management system in the classroom, and train the student in the system, providing clear descriptions of the expected behaviors and drawing up a list of privileges the student would like to earn. The goal is to eventually train the student to monitor his or her own behavior in the classroom, without constant feedback from the teacher.

SKILL UNIT 13: Leading My Learning

Targeted Skill:

Attends to task, ignores distractions.

Materials:

Leading My Learning table

Why

Many factors can play a role in a student having difficulty attending to task and ignoring distractions. Once a student's needs have been assessed, and the student has established a goal for improving on-task behavior, it is useful to implement a self-monitoring strategy. The included tools can be customized for the academic situation and the student.

How

Initially, collaborate with the student to complete these steps, but then work toward the goal of having the student manage the process for him- or herself.

1. Talk with the student about the benefits of using on-task behavior to complete work effectively and efficiently. Ask for a behavioral description of on-task behavior in the setting. Ask the student for ideas about how he or she is best able to stay on task when completing assignments. What resources help? Have the student establish a goal for increasing time on task to improve performance. Have the student rate, on a scale of 1 to 10, where he or she is currently in relation to the goal.
2. Have the student list the first small step he or she will take to work on the goal.
3. With the student, think about what materials and behaviors are necessary to begin the assignment.
4. Begin the task.
5. Periodically signal the student to observe whether he or she is on task at that moment, and note it on the card.
6. At the end of the activity, have the student or teacher (if necessary) calculate the percentage of times the student exhibited on-task behavior.
7. Finally, use a self-check or other method to check task completion and accuracy.

Name _____   Date _____

Leading My Learning

	Date _____	Date _____	Date _____	Date _____	Date _____
My goal is:					
Currently, I am at:	1 2 3 4 5 6 7 8 9 10	1 2 3 4 5 6 7 8 9 10	1 2 3 4 5 6 7 8 9 10	1 2 3 4 5 6 7 8 9 10	1 2 3 4 5 6 7 8 9 10
My step today will be to:					
To get to work, I will have to:					
On task?	☐☐☐☐☐ ☐☐☐☐	☐☐☐☐☐ ☐☐☐☐☐	☐☐☐☐☐ ☐☐☐☐☐	☐☐☐☐☐ ☐☐☐☐☐	☐☐☐☐ ☐☐☐☐
Percentage on task	___ out of ___ = ___%	___ out of ___ = ___%	___ out of ___ = ___%	___ out of ___ = ___%	___ out of ___ = ___%
Completed task accurately?	Y N Score/grade _____	Y N Score/grade _____	Y N Score/grade _____	Y N Score/grade _____	Y N Score/grade _____

© 2012 by PRO-ED, Inc.   #13936

Skill Unit 14
Respects personal boundaries, rights, and property of others

Background Information

Kids sometimes need help learning how to show respect for others. They may not recognize respectful treatment, such as taking turns, using acceptance language, waiting to talk without interrupting, or maintaining appropriate distance. School-wide and classroom-wide rules and procedures can be established to support kids in showing respect.

Respect for personal boundaries, rights, and the property of others provides the foundation for good interpersonal skills in school, at home, and in the community. People set boundaries in order to protect themselves physically, mentally, and emotionally. Cultural influences impact personal boundaries and the concepts of individual and group rights. Sometimes, students need assistance in understanding, discriminating, and accommodating others' personal boundaries. Minskoff (1980) recommended explicitly teaching students about the use of distance, spatial arrangements, and territorial concepts. She contends that although these nonverbal communication areas are less familiar to educators than the area of body language, they are of equal importance for the development of social competence.

Activities and Strategies

- Teach students four types of social distances: (a) intimate, touching up to 18 inches; (b) personal, 18 inches to 4 feet; (c) social, 4 feet to 10 feet; and (d) public, 10 feet and up. Show the length of each distance as you describe the types of situations they are used in and the relationships between people who use them. Check students' understanding after teaching the meaning of a particular distance by standing at an intimate distance from a student and ask, "Do you stand this close to a salesperson in a store?"
- Teach discrimination of spatial arrangements, such as open (informal) versus closed (formal) spatial arrangements of people (e.g., three people huddled together looking at each other vs. three people several feet apart and looking away from each other) and arrangements of furniture (e.g., straight rows vs. informal circles of chairs). Describe the behavior expected and the situations in which such a spatial arrangement would be used. Help students discriminate which situation can be joined easily and which situation cannot.
- Teach territorial concepts involving invasion of personal boundaries, invasion or avoidance of eye contact, and eavesdropping. Present two contrasting examples to demonstrate the basis for a particular territorial concept: one example in which there is an invasion of a particular territorial boundary and another in which there is respect for the boundary. For example, contrast standing on a crowded bus, touching versus not touching a stranger's hand while holding a pole; contrast a student taking a teacher's pencil from the top of her desk versus the inside of her purse; contrast staring at a stranger in a waiting

room versus looking away; or contrast a student listening to a conversation between the teacher and another student's mother versus the student engaging in a task and appearing not to listen.

- To help students grasp the idea of physical personal boundaries, play music and let them exercise with a Hula Hoop. Stop the music after a few minutes, and demonstrate how the hoop creates a circle around your body. Take the Hula Hoops away, and ask the students if they can still imagine the circle around them. Ask the students to give a definition of the word *boundary* (a line showing an area or a territory). Use features of the room or areas on a map to illustrate the concept. Explain that we all have personal boundaries or a space around us we are most comfortable keeping between us and others. Explain that we all have a right to our personal boundaries: **This means that it is not OK for someone to grab you, hit you, or otherwise invade your boundary space. We call not doing these things "respecting others' boundaries." People can come within your personal boundary space if you choose to let them, but we also have a responsibility to respect the personal boundary space of others. This means using self-control to avoid hurting someone else by inappropriately intruding on their personal boundary space by touching, hitting, or taking something from them.** Other boundary-busting behaviors include pointing your finger in someone's face, sticking your foot out in front of someone, and hugging or tickling someone when it's not welcome.
- Explain that boundaries are also fluid and can change. We have the right to choose when to let someone come close to us or when we prefer that they stay farther away. Acceptable boundaries can also vary among cultures. It is important to let people know when they are violating our personal boundaries.
- Have the students suggest a list of ways to show respect for personal boundaries, such as keeping hands and feet to themselves, staying a comfortable distance from people when talking to them, and respecting the property of others.
- In pairs, ask the students to role-play some typical situations where peoples' boundaries may be affected. Have them show a variety of verbal and nonverbal ways to respect others' boundaries and have others respect theirs. Ask them to talk about which methods worked best for them. What verbal and nonverbal signals told them the other person was uncomfortable? How can we watch others and gauge their comfort level by how close we are to them or let others know when we are uncomfortable with how close they are?
- Introduce the idea of space protection. Explain that, in general, it's not a good idea to get closer to other people than you could if you had both hands on your hips, with your elbows out (Alvord et al., 2011). Demonstrate the position. This position helps students protect their own space from invasion. Ask students what else they could do to protect their space. Suggest, **Perhaps you might say something in a firm voice, move away, or just stand tall, with shoulders back, and assert yourself, giving people a message that they are in your space.**
- Help kids who are concerned about others intruding in the space around them. Enlist the help of the students to define boundaries and to tape off the space around each desk on the floor. Have students ask each other's permission to enter the space.
- Create a climate of emotional safety by establishing classroom and school rules that encourage respect for one another.

SKILL UNIT 14: I'll Look, But I Won't Touch

Targeted Skill:

Respects personal boundaries, rights, and property of others.

Materials:

Reminder Card

Why

Students who engage in what seems like inconsequential behaviors (e.g., grabbing, picking, or taking something that belongs to someone else) can be a big deal to another, and when the behavior is perceived as disrespectful, the offended person may react very strongly. The lack of respect shown to people and their property can range from annoying behaviors, such as touching another student's back while in line, to destructive acts, as taking another's written work and tearing it up. Regardless of the severity of the action, when a student fails to respect another person, or that person' property or boundaries, conflict will usually be the end result.

How

"I'll Look, But I Won't Touch," is a simple, cognitive behavioral strategy that can help students demonstrate respect for others. Here's how it works:

1. Teach the student what the phrase, "I'll look, but I won't touch" means. Use examples from the student's experiences at school to help explain the times and places when this might be an important rule to remember. For example, in school, most people don't like it when someone
   * takes their pencils, papers, or books;
   * touches, grabs, or hits them;
   * gets too close to them, especially when they are agitated or upset; and
   * enters a private conversation unasked.

2. Discuss with the student *why* it is important to respect others, their property, their boundaries, and their rights. Talk to them about how they like to be treated, the message that it sends when someone does not respect another person, and how they would feel if other's demonstrated disrespect for them.

3. Using a *repeat, rehearse, repeat* method, teach the student to say, "I'll look, but I won't touch." Ask the student what he or she will do in various situations. Make sure that he or she repeats it out loud several times. Here are two examples:

   Adult: "You sometimes hit Joe on the arm when you pass him in the hall. He gets angry, and you two end up in a fight. What will you do instead?"
   Student: "I'll look, but I won't touch."

Adult: "If you are mad at Franco, and you see his math paper on the desk, instead of grabbing it and hiding it from him, what will you do?"

Student: "I'll look, but I won't touch."

4. Give the student a reminder card with the phrase "I'll look, but I won't touch" written on it to help the student remember. Suggest that the student put it where it will be visible throughout the day.

Just in Case

If a student has already touched another person or destroyed materials, then shoving, fighting, threatening, or something more serious might occur. If this type happens, use self-regulation and calming techniques immediately. Save the "I'll Look, But I Won't Touch" strategy for the next day, when things are calm.

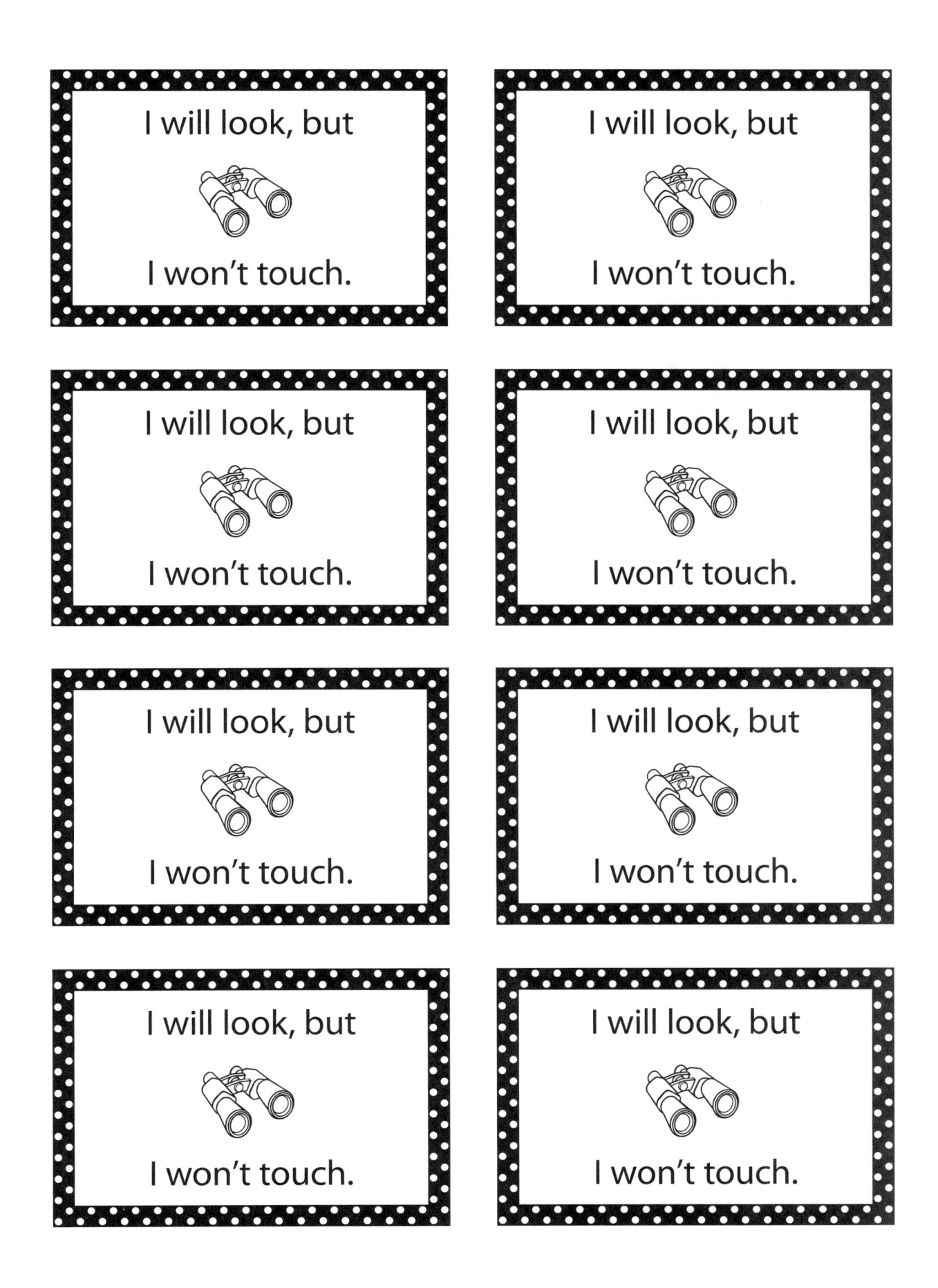

I will look, but I won't touch.	I will look, but I won't touch.
I will look, but I won't touch.	I will look, but I won't touch.
I will look, but I won't touch.	I will look, but I won't touch.
I will look, but I won't touch.	I will look, but I won't touch.

© 2012 by PRO-ED, Inc.   #13936

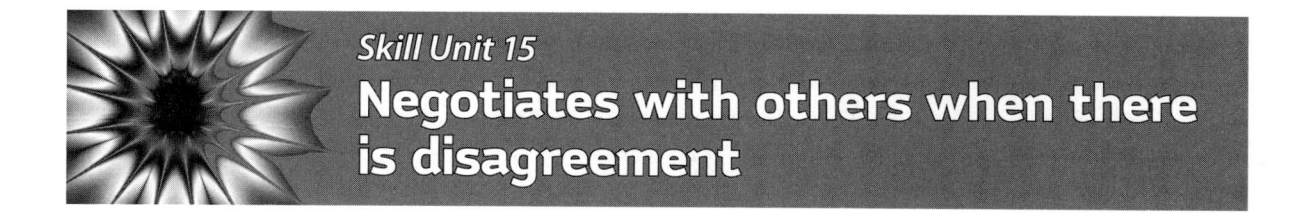

Skill Unit 15
Negotiates with others when there is disagreement

Background Information

Studies of children with heightened aggression, social rejection, depression, ADHD, or learning disabilities have generally found that they are poor at encoding social information, relatively inaccurate at detecting cues that signal a peer's intent, are more likely to label the actions of others as mean or hostile, access fewer competent responses to interpersonal problems, and generate more problematic ways of solving problems (Petti et al., 2003). These factors can definitely impact a student's ability to negotiate with others. Both adults and peers may attribute negative motivations to the sometimes awkward or incompetent behavior of students with social functioning difficulties (Galway & Metsala, 2010). One important step toward improving school social experiences for these students may be helping school personnel to better understand social cognitive functioning in general and specific areas of difficulty for any given student.

Along with addressing these factors, negotiating with others is a valuable skill that warrants teaching a negotiating/problem-solving process to all kids. Limber (2004) discouraged the use of a peer mediation or conflict resolution curriculum to address bullying because, she argues, bullying is not a conflict or a matter of occasional interpersonal disagreements but a form of chronic victimization. Limber suggest that peer mediation sends the wrong message to the bully if bullying is presented as conflict resolution (i.e., "You are both partly right and partly wrong.") These are not the times to negotiate or put two kids together to work things out. When the power differential is out of balance, the bully gains more power in a negotiation, and the victim is further victimized. Deal with bullying behavior as a disciplinary matter.

Activities and Strategies

- Get students in the habit of using one of their calming techniques before beginning a negotiating process.
- Design strategies that aim to foster more benign interpretations of others' behaviors. Ask questions such as "I'm sure you have a good reason for sensing that about the person. I wonder what else could be going on." "If it weren't that (whatever bad interpretation), how else could you choose to react?" There are lots of examples in children's literature where you can pause and discuss possible interpretations of others' behavior and help the student take various perspectives on characters' behaviors.
- Provide empathy-building experiences to view other people more benignly.
- Build recognition of responses to a problem that are most likely to be successful. Ask, "When you handled something like this before, what worked for you? How could that work here?" For younger students, calling on their Super Heroes can help. Ask, "What

would (the favorite Super Hero) recommend doing at a time like this so that everybody got what they needed and no one got hurt?"
- Once they have identified responses that might be successful, work toward competent enactment of such responses. Ask, "What's the first thing we need to do to be able to achieve that solution?" Practice the small steps first, if necessary.
- The problem-solving process is most effective when it is reinforced school-wide with specific phrasing and steps modeled for all. Typically, the problem-solving/negotiating process goes like this:
  1. State your position calmly.
  2. Let the other state his or her position.
  3. Evaluate, fairly, the other's position.
  4. Compromise.
- Psychosocial group work and ongoing coaching around these skills might benefit students who frequently have difficulty. Preventive coaching as well as in vivo support during the course of social interactions could be practiced.
- It is important to be aware of disagreements that are actually bullying situations. Avoid peer mediation or conflict resolution meetings. Apply discipline to the bully. Work with the targeted student away from the situation, in a neutral setting, and suggest, "Let's talk about an action we can take today to address the challenge of bullying that you are facing" (Blanco, 2003).
- If the disagreement is with an adult, help students learn and practice these steps (Walker, 1988):
  1. Choose or ask for a good time to talk.
  2. Be prepared to tell your side of the problem.
  3. Use a calm, respectful tone of voice.
  4. Listen to the adult's position.
  5. Come to an agreement.

SKILL UNIT 15 | I Want/You Want

Targeted Skill:

Negotiates with others when there is disagreement.

Materials:

I Want/You Want chart, I Want/You Want Self-Check

Why

Some people want their own way, all the time. While it may be difficult to negotiate, compromise, and accept not getting everything they want, students who learn these skills may be happier and more successful. Many school and workplace situations require individuals who disagree with each other to work out their differences and cooperate for the good of everyone. Mastering these skills may be a challenge for some students, but they are likely to be useful in all areas of their lives. For students whose insistence on having their own way leads to anger, aggression, or explosions, learning to compromise and negotiate is even more important.

How

The word *negotiate* means to settle a situation by discussion and mutual agreement, and *compromise* means to settle differences by each side making concessions. Both words imply that the people involved will have to give up something to come to an agreement. "I Want/You Want" is a simple and direct strategy teachers can use to teach these two skills.

1. Teach the definitions of *negotiate* and *compromise* using real-life examples. Start with situations in which people have competing interests. For young children, stick with concrete examples they can relate to easily:
   - "There is only one piece of cake and we both want it. What should we do?"
   - "We only have one TV. My sister and I have different favorite shows, and they are on at the same time. How can we resolve this issue?"
   - "My math teacher told me I have to stay after school to finish a project, but I have a part-time job. If I don't show up, I might get fired."

   After providing examples, ask the student to suggest some situations that might cause conflict or require negotiation and compromise.

2. As you explain the terms and discuss simple compromises, be sure to emphasize the negotiation aspect of the process. For example, when discussing the situations mentioned in Step 1, talk to the students not only about the outcome (the compromise) but also about how the compromise was reached (the negotiation). Explain that reaching a compromise often requires people to talk to each other and be flexible. It may also mean giving up something they want.

195 © 2012 by PRO-ED, Inc. #13936

3. Discuss the skills needed for a productive and positive negotiation. Negotiating requires good interpersonal skills, especially good communication skills. Here are some tips:
    - **Start with a positive attitude.** Smile, greet the other person, and expect a good outcome.
    - **Make sure you know what you want, and have some ideas for coming to an agreement.** Before beginning, write down some suggestions that might be part of an acceptable compromise.
    - **Look for ways to agree, and don't focus only on the areas of disagreement.** It is important not to get "stuck" on areas of disagreement. Look for any areas of agreement, no matter how small.
    - **Be honest.** Do not pretend or play games, and always tell the truth.
    - **Communicate effectively.** Stay pleasant. Rephrase, check for understanding, smile—show that positive attitude.
    - **End on a positive note.** Find areas of agreement. If you do not reach agreement, get together again and keep trying.

The student can use the "I Want/You Want Self-Check" card to evaluate his or her performance during the practice negotiations.

- Provide the student with the I Want/You Want chart. This tool is a Venn diagram, which many students will be familiar with from classroom lessons. Using the chart, provide the student with some scenarios and help him or her complete each section. Here is an example:
    - The student plays the role of a student, and the adult plays the role of the social studies teacher: **My social studies teacher always assigns me to work with Gemma. I like her okay, but she never does what she is supposed to do, and I end up doing all the work.**
    - The I Want/You Want chart would might look like this:

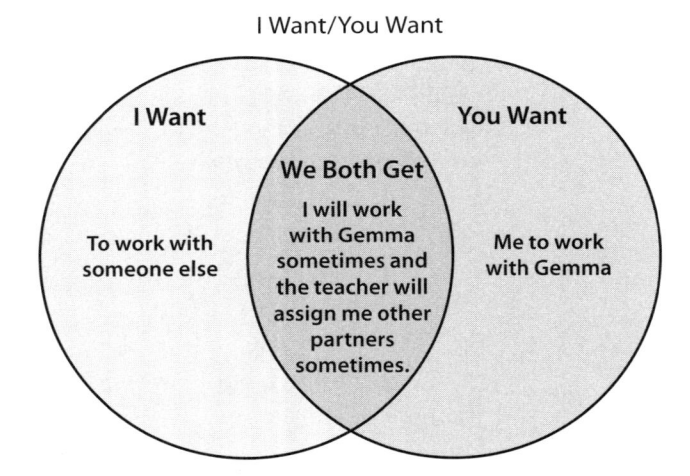

I Want/You Want

I Want: To work with someone else

We Both Get: I will work with Gemma sometimes and the teacher will assign me other partners sometimes.

You Want: Me to work with Gemma

As you work with the student to complete the chart, emphasize the do's and don'ts of good communication during the negotiation process.

Just in Case

Some students may need practice with the interpersonal skills mentioned in Step 3 *before* they start to practice negotiating and compromising. For example, if a student is hostile and negative going into a negotiation, things probably will not go well. The student also must learn to suggest solutions that may not include everything he or she wants. For students who cannot successfully negotiate because they lack these prerequisite skills, adults will need to "back up" and address those skills first.

Name _____ Date _____

I Want/You Want

I Want

You Want

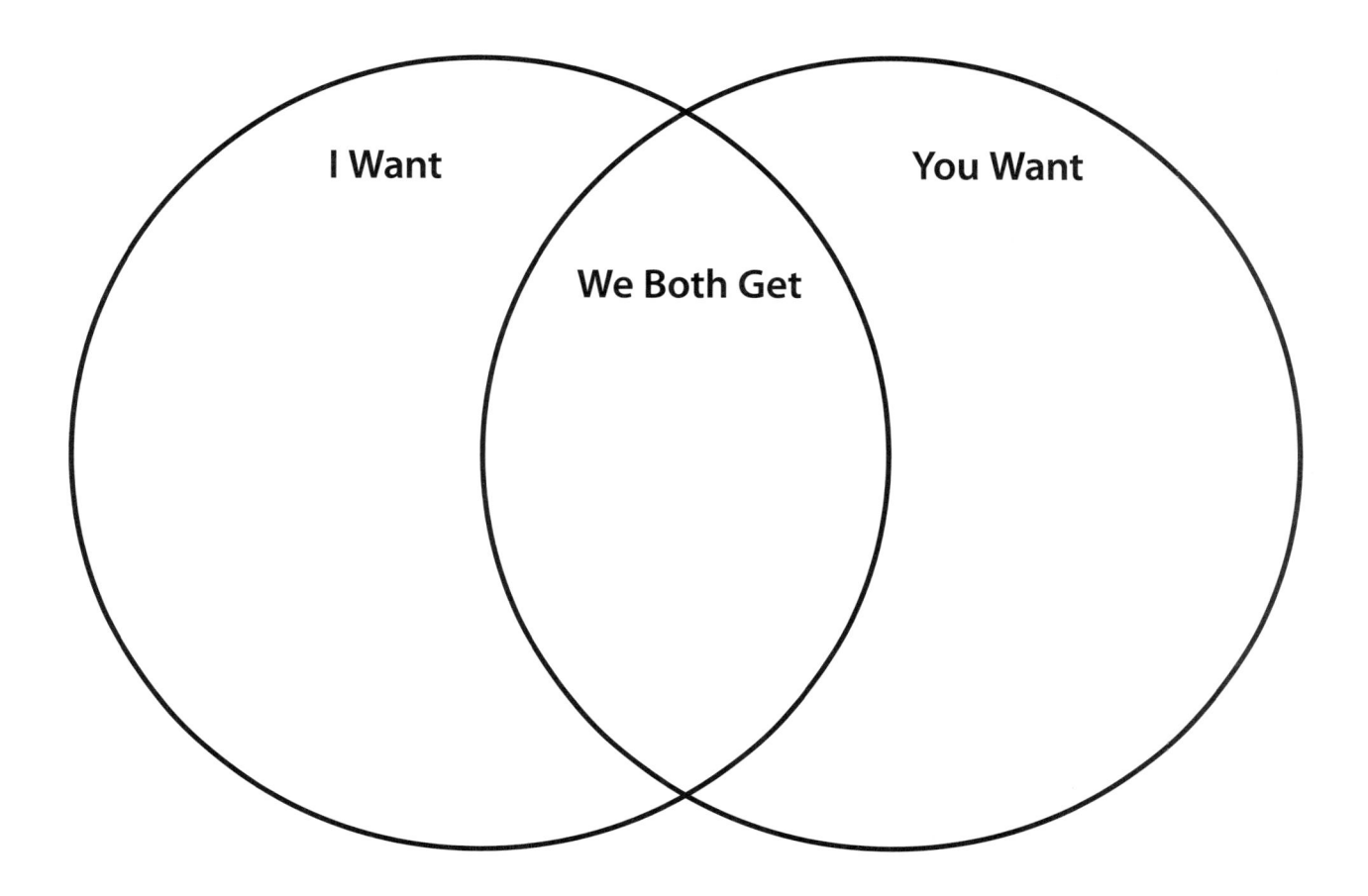

We Both Get

© 2012 by PRO-ED, Inc.   #13936

Name _____ Date _____

I Want/You Want Self-Check

Did I do well on all of these?

- ❏ ***Start with a positive attitude.*** Smile, greet the other person, and expect a good outcome.

- ❏ ***Make sure you know what you want, and have some ideas for coming to an agreement.*** Before beginning, write down some suggestions that might be part of an acceptable compromise.

- ❏ ***Look for ways to agree, and don't focus only on the areas of disagreement.*** It is important not to get "stuck" on areas of disagreement. Look for any areas of agreement, no matter how small.

- ❏ ***Be honest.*** Do not pretend or play games, and always tell the truth.

- ❏ ***Communicate effectively.*** Stay pleasant. Rephrase, check for understanding, smile—show that positive attitude.

- ❏ ***End on a positive note.*** Find areas of agreement. If you do not reach agreement, consider getting together again.

Did we reach a compromise?   YES   NO

What could I have done better?

_____

_____

© 2012 by PRO-ED, Inc.   #13936

References

Alvord, M. K., Zucker, B., & Grados, J. J. (2011). *Resilience builder program for children and adolescents: Enhancing social competence and self-regulation.* Champaign, IL: Research Press.

Bandura, A. (1986). *Social foundations of thought and action: A social cognitive theory.* Upper Saddle River, NJ: Prentice Hall.

Bear, G. G. (2011). Best practices in classroom discipline. In A. Thomas & J. Grimes (Eds.), *Best practices in school psychology V* (pp. 1403–1420). Bethesda, MD: National Association of School Psychologists.

Bear, G. G., Manning, M. A., & Izard, C. (2003). Responsible behavior: The importance of social cognition and emotion. *School Psychology Quarterly, 18,* 140–157.

Bedi, R. P., Davis, M. D., & Williams, M. (2005). Critical incidents in the formation of the therapeutic alliance from the client's perspective. *Psychotherapy: Theory, Research, Practice, Training, 42,* 311–323.

Birch, S. H., & Ladd, G. W. (1998). Children's interpersonal behaviors and teacher–child relationships. *Developmental Psychology, 34,* 934–946.

Blakemore, S. J., Rees, G., & Frith, C. D. (1998). How do we predict the consequences of our actions? A functional imaging study. *Neuropsychologia, 36*(6), 521–529.

Bray, M. A., Kehle, T. J., Caterino, L. C., & Grigerick, S. E. (2011). Best practices in the assessment and the remediation of communication disorders. In A. Thomas & J. Grimes (Eds.), *Best practices in school psychology V* (pp. 1221–1232). Bethesda, MD: National Association of School Psychologists.

Burden, P. R. (2003). *Classroom management: Creating a successful learning community* (2nd ed.). New York: John Wiley & Sons.

Cangelosi, J. S. (2000). *Classroom management strategies: Gaining and maintaining students' cooperation* (4th ed.). New York: John Wiley & Sons.

Christenson, S. L., & Peterson, C. (2008). *Parenting for school success.* St. Paul: University of Minnesota Extension.

Collaborative for Academic, Social, and Emotional Learning. (2003). *Safe and sound: An educational leader's guide to evidence-based social and emotional learning programs.* Chicago: Author.

Colvin, G., Sugai, G., Good, R., & Lee, Y. (1997). Using active supervision and precorrection to improve transition behaviors in an elementary school. *School Psychology Quarterly, 12,* 344–363.

Decety, J., & Jackson, P. L. (2004). The functional architecture of human empathy. *Behavioral and Cognitive Neuroscience Review, 3*(2), 71–100.

Dimitrovsky, L., Spector, H., Levy-Shiff, R., & Vakil, E. (1998). Interpretation of facial expressions of affect in children with learning disabilities with verbal or nonverbal deficits. *Journal of Learning Disabilities, 31,* 286–292.

References

Domagala-Zysk, E. (2006). The significance of adolescents' relationships with significant others and school failure. *School Psychology International, 27,* 232–247.

DuPaul, G. J., Stoner, G., & O'Reilly, M. J. (2011). Best practices in classroom interventions for attention problems. In A. Thomas & J. Grimes (Eds.), *Best practices in school psychology V* (pp. 1421–1437). Bethesda, MD: National Association of School Psychologists.

Elias, M. J., Tobias, S. E., & Friedlander, B. S. (1999). *Emotionally intelligent parenting: How to raise a self-disciplined, responsible, socially skilled child.* New York: Three Rivers Press.

Fisher, J., & Ogden, P. (2009). Sensorimotor psychotherapy. In C. Courtois & J. D. Ford (Eds.), *Treating complex traumatic stress disorders: An evidence-based guide.* New York: Guilford Press.

Ford, J. D., & Cloitre, M. (2009). Best practices in psychotherapy for children and adolescents. In C. A. Courtois & J. D. Ford (Eds.), *Treating complex traumatic stress disorders: An evidence-based guide* (pp. 59–81). New York: Guilford Press.

Fosha, D. (2003). Dyadic regulation and experiential work with emotion and relatedness in trauma and disorganized attachment. In M. F. Soloman & D. J. Siegel (Eds.), *Healing trauma* (pp. 221–281). New York: Norton.

Galway, T. M., & Metsala, J. L. (2010). Social cognition and its relation to psychosocial adjustment in children with nonverbal learning disabilities. *Journal of Learning Disabilities, 44,* 33–49.

Gettinger, M., & Ball, C. (2011). Best practices in increasing academic engaged time. In A. Thomas & J. Grimes (Eds.), *Best practices in school psychology V* (pp. 1043–1057). Bethesda, MD: National Association of School Psychologists.

Grusec, J. E., & Goodnow, J. J. (1994). Impact of parental discipline methods on the child's internalization of values: A reconceptualization of current points of view. *Developmental Psychology, 30,* 4–19.

Hamre, B. K., & Pianta, R. C. (2006). Student-teacher relationships. In G. C. Bear & K. M. Minke (Eds.), *Children's needs III: Development, prevention, and intervention* (pp. 49–59). Bethesda, MD: National Association of School Psychologists.

Henderlong, J., & Lepper, M. R. (2002). The effects of praise on student's intrinsic motivation: A review and synthesis. *Psychological Bulletin, 128*(5), 774–795.

Kern, L., Dunlap, G., Childs, K., & Clarke, S. (1994). Use of a class-wide self-management program to improve the behavior of students with emotional and behavioral disorders. *Education and Treatment of Children, 17,* 445–458.

Kestenbaum, R., Farber, E. A., & Sroufe, L. A. (1989). Individual differences in empathy among preschoolers: Relation to attachment history. *New Directions for Child Development, 44,* 51–64.

Kutz, D. (2009). *Seclusions and Restraints: Selected Cases of Death and Abuse at Public and Private Schools and Treatment Centers.* Washington, DC: US GAO. www.gao.gov/products/GAO-09-719T

Lam, A. L., Cole, C. L., Shapiro, E. S., & Bambara, L. M. (1994). Relative effects of self-monitoring on-task behavior, academic accuracy, and disruptive behavior in students with behavior disorders. *School Psychology Review, 23,* 44–58.

Lantieri, L. (2008). *Building emotional intelligence.* Boulder, CO: Sounds True.

References

Levine, P. A. (1997). *Waking the tiger: Healing trauma.* Berkeley, CA: North Atlantic Books.

Levine, P. A., & Kline, M. (2007). *Trauma through a child's eyes.* Berkeley, CA: North Atlantic Books.

Lewis, T., Sugai, G., & Colvin, G. (2000). The effects of pre-corrective active supervision on the recess behavior of elementary students. *Education and Treatment of Children, 23*(2), 109–121.

Limber, S. P. (2004). Implementation of the Olweus bullying prevention program in American schools: Lessons learned from the field. In D. L. Espelage & S. M. Swearer (Eds.), *Bullying in American schools* (pp. 351–364). Mahwah, NJ: Erlbaum.

Lynch, E. W., & Hanson, M. J. (Eds.). (2004). *Developing cross-cultural competence: A guide for working with children and their families* (3rd ed.). Baltimore: Brookes.

McConnell, K., Ryser, G., & Patton, J. P. (2010a). *Practical ideas that really work for students with disruptive, defiant, or difficult behaviors: PreK–grade 4* (2nd ed.). Austin, TX: PRO-ED.

McConnell, K., Ryser, G., & Patton, J. P. (2010b). *Practical ideas that really work for students with disruptive, defiant, or difficult behaviors: Grades 5–12* (2nd ed.). Austin, TX: PRO-ED.

Minskoff, E. H. (1980). Teaching approach for developing nonverbal communication skills in students with social perception deficits: Part II. Proxemics, vocalic, and artifactual cues. *Journal of Learning Disabilities, 13,* 203–208.

Mueller, C. M., & Dweck, C. S. (1998). Praise for intelligence can undermine student's motivation and performance. *Journal for Personality and Social Psychology, 75*(1), 33–52.

Murphy, J. J. (2008). *Solution focused counseling in the schools* (2nd ed.). Alexandria, VA: American Counseling Association.

National Disability Rights Network. (2009, January). *School is not supposed to hurt: Investigative report on abusive restraint and seclusion in schools.* Washington, DC: Author.

Nowicki, S., Jr., & Duke, M. (1992). The association of children's nonverbal decoding abilities with their popularity, locus of control, and academic achievement. *Journal of Genetic Psychology, 153,* 385–393.

Ogden, P., Minton, K., & Pain, C. (2006). *Trauma and the body.* New York: Norton.

Olson, J. L., & Platt, J. M. (2000). *Teaching children and adolescents with special needs* (3rd ed.). Upper Saddle River, NJ: Merrill.

Pepler, D., Jiang, D., Craig, W., & Connolly, J. (2008). Developmental trajectories of bullying and associated factors. *Child Development, 79*(2), 335–338.

Perry, B. D. (2006). Applying principles of neurodevelopment to clinical work with maltreated and traumatized children. In N. Boyd (Ed.), *Working with traumatized youth in child welfare* (pp. 27–52). New York: Guilford Press.

Petti, V., Voelker, S., Shore, D., & Hayman-Abello, S. (2003). Perception of nonverbal emotional cues by children with nonverbal learning disabilities. *Journal of Developmental and Physical Disabilities, 23,* 23–36.

Pizarro, D. A., & Salovey, P. (2002). Being and becoming a good person: The role of emotional intelligence in moral development and behavior. In J. Aronson (Ed.), *Improving academic achievement: Impact of psychological factors on education.* San Diego, CA: Academic Press.

Rothschild, B. (2000). *The body remembers: The psychophysiology of trauma and trauma treatment* (pp. 78–80). New York: Norton.

References

Rothschild, B. (2003). *The body remembers casebook.* New York: Norton.

Rourke, B. P. (1995). Introduction: The NLD syndrome and the white matter model. In B. P. Rourke (Ed.), *Syndrome of nonverbal learning disabilities: Neurodevelopmental manifestations* (pp. 1–26). New York: Guilford Press.

Ryan, J. B., Peterson, R. L., Tetreault, G., & van der Hagen, E. (2007). Reducing the use of seclusion and restraint in a day school program. In M. A. Nunno, L. Bullard, & D. M. Day (Eds.), *For our own good: Examining the safety of high-risk interventions for children and young people* (pp. 201–216) Washington, DC: Child Welfare League of America.

Saxe, G., Ellis, B., & Kaplow, J. (2007). *Collaborative treatment of traumatized children and teens.* New York: Guilford Press.

Schore, A. (2003). *Affect regulation and the origin of the self.* Hillsdale, NJ: Erlbaum.

Schumacher, E. H., Seymour, T. L., Glass, J. M., Fencsik, D. E., Lauber, E. J., Kieras, D. E., & Meyer, D. E. (2001). Virtually perfect time sharing in dual-task performance: Uncorking the central cognitive bottleneck. *Psychological Science: Special Issue, 121*(2), 2101–2108.

Siegel, D. J. (1999). *The developing mind: Toward a neurobiology of interpersonal experience.* New York: Guilford Press.

Siegel, D. J. (2003). An interpersonal neurobiology of psychotherapy: The developing mind and the resolution of trauma. In M. F. Soloman & D. J. Siegel (Eds.), *Healing trauma* (pp. 1–56). New York: Norton.

Siegel, D. J. (2007). *Being present in body and mind: An integration of clinical treatment and neuroscience research* [CD]. Los Angeles: Lifespan Learning Institute.

Smith, T. E. C., Polloway, E. A., Patton, J. R., & Dowdy, C. A. (2001). *Teaching students with special needs in inclusive settings* (3rd ed.). Boston: Allyn & Bacon.

Tollison, P. K., Synatschk, K. O., & Logan, G. (2011). *Self-regulation for kids k–12: Strategies for calming minds and behavior.* Austin, TX: PRO-ED.

U.S. Department of Education. (2010, February). *Summary of seclusion and restraint statutes, regulations, policies and guidance, by state and territory: Information as reported to the regional comprehensive center and gathered from other sources.* Washington, DC: Author.

Van der Kolk, B. A. (2006). Clinical implications of neuroscience research in PTSD. *Annals New York Academy of Sciences, 1071,* 277–293.

Van der Kolk, B. A. (2007). *New frontiers in trauma treatment.* Portola Valley, CA: Institute for the Advancement of Human Behavior.

Wallace, A. (2006). *The attention revolution: Unlocking the power of the focused mind.* Somerville, MA: Wisdom.

Zimmerman, B. J., Greenberg, D., & Weinstein, C. E. (1994). Self-regulating academic study time: A strategy approach. In D. H. Schunk & B. J. Zimmerman (Eds.), *Self-regulation of learning and performance: Issues and educational applications* (pp. 181–199). Hillsdale, NJ: Erlbaum.

Zins, J. E., Weissberg, R. P., Wang, M. C., & Walberg, H. J. (2004). *Building academic success on social and emotional learning: What does the research say?* New York: Teachers College Press.

About the Authors

Kathleen McConnell, PhD, is an independent education consultant and coauthor of a wide range of materials for educators, including the *Practical Ideas That Really Work* series. She has experience as a general education teacher, special education teacher, and college professor in teacher preparation programs. Kathy provides consultation, staff development, and support in the areas of behavior intervention, autism, and effective instruction in inclusive environments. She likes to help educators find positive, practical approaches to challenging situations. In addition to her individual consultation, Kathy often works with a team of other professionals to complete special and general education program reviews in school districts nationwide.

Katherine O. Synatschk, PhD, LPCS, has been involved with counseling as a professional school counselor, director of counseling, licensed professional counselor in private practice, counselor educator, school social worker, and special education teacher. She trains counselors and educators at the national and international levels. She coauthored, with Patricia K. Tollison, *SOS! A Practical Guide for Leading Solution-Focused Groups,* and *Self-Regulation for Kids K–12: Strategies for Calming Minds and Behavior.* She is currently an adjunct associate professor at Texas State University and the executive editor at PRO-ED, Inc.